# What the Cults Believe

## *Fourth Edition, Revised*

*By*

IRVINE ROBERTSON

MOODY PRESS
CHICAGO

*128057*

Fourth Edition, 1983

Library of Congress Cataloging in Publication Data
Robertson, Irvine.
    What the cults believe
    Bibliography: p. 169.
    1. Cults—United States.  2. Christian Sects—United States.
I. Title.
BL2530.U6R62        1979          291.2        79-18219
ISBN 0-8024-9411-0

15 16 17 Printing/GB/Year 87 86 85 84

*Printed in the United States of America*

*To my beloved and our stalwart four*

# *Preface*

THE PHENOMENAL RISE of the cults has been one of the characteristics of the second half of the twentieth century. An estimated 3,000 cults claim followers in the United States, with overflow into Canada. The witnessing and proselytizing zeal of many of these movements poses a continuing threat to the believing Christian. Perhaps *threat* is not the proper word, because neither the Christian message nor position in Christ are in any way threatened. But there is the constant *challenge* of the cultist and his apparent success, so that the nominal Christian (and even the untaught believer) is a potential prey to the purveyor of "new truth." Such so-called truth presents variously defined ways of salvation that appeal to the flesh.

With sufficient truth, or pseudotruth, to deceive, the cults demand a commitment that is total, and they prescribe a constant round of activity that gives apparent satisfaction to those who prefer the way of works to the way of faith (Prov. 14:12). An understanding of the historical backgrounds and major teachings of these groups is imperative for an effective and aggressive Christian witness. Emphasis on the history of the cults will be minor, with attention mainly focused on the teachings.

This revision contains the salient features of the cults, as did the first writing. However, the format is different, and much material has been added. A new introduction has been included—one that contains a more detailed basic

9

definition of a cult and a more complete list of suggestions for dealing with cult members. Today we do not speak of "the four major cults"—as if the field of cultism were so limited. Certainly the Worldwide Church of God, the Unification Church, and more recently The Way International have come into places of considerable influence. Christian Science does not appear to have maintained its position of major outreach.

A new section has been included that deals with the fundamental teachings of Eastern mysticism. Major movements and their distinctives are considered, albeit the source and basics are really the same for all of them. Also, a new section has been added on the major doctrinal deviations of the cults.

# Introduction

"Now THE SPIRIT speaketh expressly, that in the latter times some shall depart from the faith, giving heed to seducing spirits, and doctrines of devils; speaking lies in hypocrisy" (1 Tim. 4:1-2*a*).

Current cult methods of attacking truth fall into two main classifications. The first is an appeal to pride through rationalistic philosophy. The second demands a credulity that is akin to superstition, and calls it "faith." A common cult feature is the denial, in whole or in part, of the deity of Jesus Christ. "This is that spirit of antichrist [which is], in the world" (1 John 4:3). It impugns both Christ's person and His work. As Samuel Zwemer once said about Islam, "It gives Him a place by displacing Him."

Just what is a cult? Webster's dictionary gives the authoritative definition, which reads in part: "A system of religious beliefs and ritual; a religion regarded as unorthodox or spurious; great devotion to a person, idea, or thing." *Sect* may be regarded as a synonym. Charles S. Braden gives this precise definition: "A cult, as I define it, is any religious group which differs significantly in some one or more respects as to belief or practise from those religious groups which are regarded as the normative expressions of religion in our total culture."[1] This is all-inclusive, and well stated. It includes both pseudo-Christian and non-Christian cults. It might be added that in many cultic move-

1. C. S. Braden, *These Also Believe* (New York: Macmillan, 1949), p. xii.

11

ments, there is often a charismatic leader who is a strong authority figure.

Cults active today may be divided into at least four classifications, with considerable overlapping.

1. *Pseudo-Christian cults.* Walter R. Martin defines these groups as those that "adhere to doctrines which are pointedly contradictory to orthodox Christianity and which yet claim the distinction of either tracing their origin to orthodox sources or of being in essential harmony with those sources."[2] In other words, a pseudo-Christian cult is one that claims to be Christian, but is not. Boasting of acceptance of Bible authority, these cults have their own writings that are interpretive of the Bible, and actually supersede it in ultimate authority. Generally claiming to be *the* true church, providing the only way of salvation, the pseudo-Christian cults profess to have recovered long-lost truth taught by the early church. Or the claim might be made that the founder has received revelation from God of truth never before known.

2. *Cults that are distinctly Eastern.* Our scientific age is seeing a revival of ancient Eastern mysticism. This mysticism is mainly Hindu, but Buddhism is also rising in several of its many varied forms. The Perennial Philosophy of ancient India is by far the most proliferated, with international organizations and local "swamis" found in many cities. These Eastern religions claim approximately a half million members in the United States. If included, interested spectators and experimenters would swell that estimated total by several million. Youth predominates, as the self- (or Self-) centered search for "truth, consciousness,

2. Walter R. Martin, *The Rise of the Cults* (Grand Rapids: Zondervan, 1955), pp. 11-12.

and bliss." Hindu-related cults usually acknowledge the Bible as one of the holy scriptures of mankind, but give it at best a minor consideration. The Hindu scriptures, *Bhagavad Gita,* and *Upanishads,* are the basic source of teaching. All Eastern cults hold to such fundamentals as monism, reincarnation, and an ultimate absorption into the "deity" that is in all and is all.

3. *Christian-Hindu cults.* These have interpreted the Bible according to Hindu teaching and are not new. Dr. Anthony A. Hoekema, in his excellent book, *The Four Major Cults,* put it most succinctly. "Christian Scientists have no more right to apply to themselves the title Christian than have Buddhists or Hindus—with those teachings, indeed, Christian Science has greater affinity than with those of Christianity."[3] In our study, several others will be considered, such as Theosophy, Unity, and so forth.

4. *Personality cults.* These gather around a single authoritative leader or founder. Such groups tend to be more ephemeral, fading away upon the death of the leader. They do not have noteworthy permanence, nor do they normally present any new, distinctive teaching.

Other cult groupings are possible, such as those with strong ethnic or cultural emphases. But our consideration will deal mainly with the cults that are pseudo-Christian, and with others that impinge upon the true Christian as well as the nominal Christian. In presenting the heresies taught by the major cults, the false teachings of the lesser cults will be covered in principle.

### Dealing with a Cultist

Usually the cultist will make the approach. A pair of Jehovah's Witnesses, or neatly dressed, young Mormon missionaries may visit your home. Regardless of where or

3. Anthony A. Hoekema, *The Four Major Cults* (Grand Rapids: Eerdmans, 1963), p. 221.

when or how a discussion may arise, write this down in
your mental notebook and underline it: *Quickly move into
command of the conversation.* Steer the discussion; ask the
questions; use the Scriptures. Here is where a knowledge
of the cultic beliefs is indispensable. Forewarned is forearmed. The deluded one with whom you talk is forearmed
indeed, but he is usually unprepared to meet questions not
covered in the outline and verses that he has memorized.
*Answer a question with another question.* Here are several
basic suggestions:

1. *Do not argue.* Avoid anything that even sounds like
an argument. This may be difficult at times, but strive to
maintain at least an appearance of respect for the beliefs
of the other person. You may despise them, but he has a
right to them.

2. *Do not ridicule the cultist.* Remember that he is desperately sincere in his beliefs. They have eternal signifi-
cance to him. Love the one who is so grievously deceived.

3. *Do not denigrate the character of the cult's founder.*
Such a tactic will only cause resentment and raise another
barrier between you and the one to whom you witness.

4. *Use the Word of God.* It is "quick and powerful"
(Heb. 4:12). Your knowledge of the Word will be more
effective than anything else in silencing and convincing the
deceived one of the truth of the gospel. But remember that
proof texts are not disproved by other proof texts. A knowledge of the immediate and remote contexts of the texts
used by the cultist will often provide the means whereby
the conversation can be steered into positive channels.

5. *Give your own testimony.* The point of any testimony
should be the impact of Christ on the life of the individual.
"This is what God has done for all men. This is what He
has done for me—and wants to do for you." There is actually no denial of a clear-cut personal testimony.

6. *Exalt the Lord Jesus Christ.* "This is My beloved Son, in whom I am well-pleased" was a repeated expression of the Father (e.g., Matt. 3:17; 17:5). He purposes to sum up all things in the Son (Eph. 1:10) and has given Him the name which is above every name (Phil. 2:9-11).

7. *Depend consciously upon the Holy Spirit.* He will surely guide and control you, to the glory of the Son. (See John 16:13-14.)

8. *Know what the cultist believes.* A knowledge of the cultist's beliefs, with a knowledge of the key texts so often quoted, will enable you (guided by the Holy Spirit) to disrupt his prepared presentation. But it also will provide for you the continued opportunity to steer the conversation along positive lines. It is hoped the conversation will not only silence his witness, but that it also will win him to a saving knowledge of our blessed Lord Jesus Christ.

# Major Doctrines of Orthodox Christianity

### THE SOURCE OF AUTHORITY

A COMPOSITE doctrinal statement from evangelical sources would include the declaration that the Bible, consisting of the sixty-six books of the Old and New Testaments, is a divine revelation, of which the original manuscripts were verbally inspired by the Holy Spirit. The Bible is absolute in its authority, complete in its revelation, final in its content, and without any errors in its statements. In the Bible is contained all that is necessary for the service of God and for our salvation. It is therefore the supreme and final authority in all matters of faith and conduct, and is the only rule and norm by which all teaching is to be judged. (See Isa. 8:19-20; Luke 16:29-31; Gal. 1:8-9; 2 Tim. 3:15-17; and 2 Peter 1:21.)

### THE DOCTRINE OF GOD

The belief of traditional Christianity is given in the *Westminster Shorter Catechism* (Question 6): "There are three persons in the Godhead; the Father, the Son, and the Holy Ghost; and these three are one God, the same in substance, equal in power and glory." (See Deut. 6:4; Jer. 10:10; Matt. 3:16-17; 28:19; and 2 Cor. 13:14.)

### THE DOCTRINE OF JESUS CHRIST

Most important in the message of the gospel are the person and work of our Lord Jesus Christ. "What think ye of Christ?" (Matt. 22:42). The answer to that question will frequently indicate veracity or heresy in any system that allies itself with Christianity.

16

Jesus Christ is the image of the invisible God, perfect in Godhood and perfect in manhood. One with the Father from eternity, He took upon Himself the nature of man, and was conceived by the Holy Ghost and born of the virgin Mary. Having died on the cross as a substitutionary sacrifice for sin, He rose from the dead in the same body that was laid to rest in the tomb. He ascended into heaven in that glorified body, and is now there interceding in behalf of all who believe in Him. He will come again, personally, bodily, and visibly, to judge the living and the dead, and to set up His Kingdom. (See Matt. 1:18-25; Luke 24; Acts 2:31-36; Phil. 2:5-8; Col. 1:15-18; 1 Thess. 4:16-18; Heb. 4:14-16; 1 Pet. 2:24-25; Rev. 11:15-17; 20:4-6, 11-15.)

## THE DOCTRINE OF MAN

After God had made all other creatures, He created man, male and female. He formed the body of the man of the dust of the ground, and the woman from a rib of the man. He endued them with living, reasonable, and immortal souls. Made after God's own image, in knowledge, righteousness, and holiness, they had the law of God written in their hearts, with power to fulfill it, yet they were subject to fall. They were given dominion over the fish of the sea, the birds of the air, and every living creature on earth.

Our first parents, being left to the freedom of their own will, fell from the estate wherein they were created, by sinning against God (Gen. 3:6-13; 2 Cor. 11:3). All mankind, descending from Adam by ordinary generation, sinned in him, and fell with him in his first transgression (Gen. 2:17; Acts 17:26; Rom. 5:12-20; 1 Cor. 15:21-22). Thus all mankind, having lost communion with God, are under His wrath and curse, and so are made liable to all miseries in this life, to death itself, and to the pains of hell forever (Rom. 5:14; 6:23; Eph. 2:3).

At death, the souls of the believers enter into the presence of Christ (Luke 23:43; John 14:3; 2 Cor. 5:1-8; Phil. 1:23); the souls of the wicked are in immediate torment (Luke 16:22-23; 2 Pet. 2:9); while bodies rest in the grave until the time of the resurrections (Rom. 8:23; 1 Thess. 4:14-18). There will be a resurrection of the just unto life, and of the wicked unto eternal damnation (John 5:28-29; 1 Thess. 4:14-18; Rev. 20:4-15).

### The Doctrine of Salvation, or the Atonement

Salvation is by grace, a gift of God, through faith in the Lord Jesus Christ. He died a voluntary death upon the cross as a substitutionary sacrifice for sin (1 Cor. 15:3; 1 Peter 2:23-24). Those who receive Christ by faith have their sins forgiven (Eph. 1:7); are born of the Spirit, thus becoming children of God (John 1:12-13); and are made new creatures in Christ Jesus (2 Cor. 5:17).

### The Doctrine of Eschatology, or Things to Come

Jesus Christ will come again personally, bodily, and visibly. At His appearance, the dead in Christ will rise first. Together with the living saints, they will be changed and caught up to meet the Lord "in the air." This is known as the rapture of the saints (1 Thess. 4:16-17; see also 1 Cor. 15:51-58). The Great Tribulation follows (the seventieth week of Daniel 9), and ends with the appearance of the Lord with His saints for judgment of peoples on earth (the revelation of Jesus Christ). Thereafter, He will set up His Kingdom, which will endure for 1,000 years (the Millennium).[1] During this period Satan will be bound, and there

1. This is the pre-Tribulation position. It is recognized that numerous orthodox, evangelical Christians hold that the second coming of Christ is altogether subsequent to the Tribulation period. Their position, known as the post-Tribulation position, maintains that both the rapture of the church and the revelation of Christ in person to set up His Kingdom occur in swift succession *after* the Tribulation.

will be universal peace and prevailing righteousness on earth. At the end of the millennial reign of Christ, Satan will be released for a short time, will wage final war against the Lord, and will be cast with his cohorts into the eternal lake of fire. There will be a resurrection of the wicked (the second resurrection), and the judgment of the great white throne will follow. All whose names are not found in the Lamb's book of life will be cast into the lake of fire for eternal punishment. (See Matt. 24:29-30; 26:64; Acts 1:11; 1 Thess. 4:16; 2 Thess. 2:7-8; and Rev. 1:7; 20:1-6, 11-15.) The saints will spend eternity with the Lord.

# Cult Deviations from Major Orthodox Doctrines

THE END OR AIM of religion is salvation. Salvation, variously defined, usually includes deliverance from the griefs, pains, and sorrows common in this life, and entrance into an ideal state of conscious, happy, and eternal existence.

Faith is acclaimed by the cults as primary and essential for salvation. Christian cults unite in preaching salvation by faith in Jesus Christ. A cursory examination reveals, however, that they offer salvation on the basis of faith *plus* continuing works. And their very concept of salvation by faith in Jesus Christ breaks down when it is seen to be connected with a denial of the deity of Christ. By this denial, the doctrine of the atonement is impugned. According to the Word of God, there is no atonement for the sins of mankind if Jesus Christ is not the eternal Son of the infinite and holy God, coequal in all things.

Four doctrines from among those considered fundamental and mandatory in orthodox Christianity are falsely taught by most cults:

> The doctrine of the Trinity
> The deity of Jesus Christ
> The personality of the Holy Spirit
> The immortality of the soul.

A fifth matter, eschatology, or the doctrine of last things, also will be considered. Recognizing that there are differences among Bible-believing people concerning the precise order of coming events, the main items emphasized by the major cults will simply be noted.

## THE DOCTRINE OF THE TRINITY

Any consideration of the doctrine of the Trinity necessarily involves study of the deity of Christ and the personality of the Holy Spirit. These will be considered subsequently under separate headings.

However, the very concept of trinity, "three persons, the same in substance, equal in power and glory," is vehemently rejected by the cults as being heathenish and unscriptural. It also is considered unreasonable, or contrary to reason, and therefore totally unacceptable. It must be readily admitted that the Trinity is a mystery, and that the term is not in the Bible. But the Bible is replete with the concept, beginning with the use of the plural noun *Elohim* (God) in Genesis 1:1. *Similar personal attributes of deity are ascribed consistently to Father, Son, and Holy Spirit.*

Dr. Merrill F. Unger writes:

> Although the doctrine of the Trinity is implicit rather than explicit in the Old Testament, at the same time, it is properly held that with the accompanying light of the New Testament this truth can be found in the Old (e.g., Num. 6:24-26; Isa. 6:3; 63:9, 10, the sanctity of the symbolical number three—the plural form of Elohim, also places [in the Old Testament] in which the deity is spoken of as conversing with himself [see Gen. 1:26; 3:22; 11:7; Isa. 6:8]. ... The same worship is paid, the same works are ascribed to each of these three persons, and in such a way as to indicate that these three are united in the fullness of the one living God. The Monotheism of the Old Testament is maintained, while glimpses are nevertheless, afforded into the tripersonal mode of the divine existence.[1]

1. Merrill F. Unger, "Trinity," in *Unger's Bible Dictionary,* ed. Merrill F. Unger (Chicago: Moody, 1966), p. 1118.

Antitrinitarian teaching is by no means a new heresy. The early church met it and answered it in the great church councils of that period. It is helpful to read the creeds of the early church in this regard. (See any major church history textbook on the creeds of Christendom.)

## THE DEITY OF JESUS CHRIST

The full deity of the Son is, of course, contained within the doctrine of the Trinity. And all the pseudo-Christian cults categorically reject this truth. His oneness, or equality, with the Father will be the focus of considerable attack by the cultist. Christ, they declare, is the first-born of God; the only direct creation of God; the one by whom all else was created; uniquely born; sinless; a miracle worker; the only efficacious sacrifice—but *not* equal with the Father.

Equality with the Father and oneness with Him in all things was unquestionably claimed by Jesus Christ and consistently ascribed to Him by the New Testament writers. The gospel of John was written to prove that Jesus was the Christ, the Son of God (John 20:31). As such, He was coequal with the Father. The Jewish leaders of that day rightly understood His claim and determined to kill Him for that reason (see John 5:17-18). Jesus did not deny their understanding, but rather verified it extensively in His response (John 5:19-32). John's gospel concludes with the ultimate in worship, expressed by the apostle Thomas in the upper room when he said to Jesus, "My Lord and My God" (John 20:28).

The importance of this doctrine cannot be overstated. Because the very doctrine of the atonement depends on this eternal truth, the following verses are set forth to bolster further the correct view of this doctrine.

*Philippians 2:6.* The word *form,* as used in this verse (NASB), does not refer to outward shape or appearance.

It indicates that which is intrinsic and essential. Other excellent translations make this clear: "being in very nature God" (*New International Version*); "His state was divine" (*Jerusalem Bible*). J. B. Phillips so plainly renders it, "who had always been God by nature." These and other reputable translations declare that Jesus Christ is divine by nature. Divinity was not something He acquired. It was His from eternity. He was in the beginning, He was with God, He was God.

*Colossians 1:15 and Hebrews 1:3.* Two Greek words are translated by the English *image* in these verses. Christ is declared to be "the image of the invisible God," and "the exact representation of His nature." In Colossians 1:15 the word is *eikon*, referring to "moral likeness," or Christ's conformity to God in moral excellence or holiness. In Hebrews 1:3 the word is *charakter*, easily recognizable as the English *character*. However, it signifies the "exact impression" of any person or thing, such as the imprint left by a metal stamp. Christ, it declares, is the precise facsimile of God in every aspect. "He who has seen me," Jesus said, "has seen the Father" (John 14:9). Jesus Christ perfectly reflects the glory and majesty of God, for He is God. It does not take a knowledge of Greek to make use of such obvious and significant declarations from Scripture.

At times the cultist will refer to Colossians 1:15 to prove that Christ is "the first created being," therefore inferior to the Father. Note carefully this quotation from Dr. Metzger's precise and scholarly comment:

> Actually the verb "to create" in reference to the relation of the Son of God to the Father appears neither here nor anywhere in the New Testament. Here he is spoken of as "the first begotten of all creation," which is something quite different from saying that he was made or created. . . . To return to Col. 1:15 where Paul speaks of

Christ as "the first begotten of all creation," it is important
to observe that the adjective "first" refers both to rank as
well as time. In other words, the Apostle alludes here not
only to Christ's *priority* to all creation, but also to his
*sovereignty* over all creation.

Later in the Epistle to the Colossians (2:9) Paul declares, "It is in him (Jesus Christ) that all the fullness of
the divine quality dwells bodily". . . . Nothing could be
clearer or more emphatic than this declaration. It means
that everything without exception which goes to make up
the godhead, or divine quality, dwells or resides in Jesus
Christ bodily, that is, is invested with a body in Jesus
Christ. It is to be noticed also that Paul uses the present
tense of the verb, "dwells." He does not say that the fullness of the divine quality "has dwelt" or "will dwell" in
Jesus Christ, but that it "dwells" there. All that the creeds
of the Church mean by speaking of Jesus Christ as *eternally* the only begotten Son of the Father is contained in
Paul's deliberate use of the present tense of the verb
"dwells."[2]

An additional argument might be found in Hebrews 1:3,
which states that Christ is "the radiance [or outshining] of
His glory." His glory! What is the glory of God? It is the
sum total of His attributes. God's glory is what God is. And
Christ is the effulgence or outshining of that glory. What
more can be said? F. F. Bruce writes, "Just as the glory is
really in the effulgence, so the substance of God is really in
Christ, who is its impress, its exact representation and em-
bodiment. What God essentially is, is made manifest in
Christ. To see Christ is to see what the Father is like."[3]

### THE PERSONALITY OF THE HOLY SPIRIT

Many of those who reject the biblical concept of the

2. Bruce M. Metzger, *The Jehovah's Witnesses and Jesus Christ* (Princeton, N.J.: Theological Book Agency), pp. 77, 78.
3. F. F. Bruce, *Commentary on the Epistle to the Hebrews* (Grand Rapids: Eerdmans, 1964), p. 6.

Trinity reduce the Holy Spirit to an "influence," or "power of God, not a person."

Beginning with Genesis 1:2, the Holy Spirit is depicted as working with the Father and the Son in creation and the affairs of mankind. In the upper room discourse, His coming was foretold by Christ. "I will ask the Father," said the Lord, "and He will give you another Helper, that He may be with you forever; that is the Spirit of truth . . . you know Him because He abides with you, and will be in you" (John 14:16-17). See John 14-16 for the whole context. Taking the place of the Son, the Holy Spirit was to continue the work that Jesus "began to do and teach, until the day when He was taken up" (Acts 1:1-2*a*). In Acts the Spirit is seen founding the church, empowering the disciples, and leading in the expansion of the church unto the uttermost part of the world.

His many titles indicate His deity and His relationship with the Father and the Son. He is called:

> The Spirit of Knowledge—Isaiah 11:2
> The Spirit of Truth—John 14:17
> The Spirit of Holiness—Romans 1:4
> The Spirit of God—Genesis 1:2
> The Spirit of Christ—Romans 8:9
> The Spirit of the Lord—Acts 5:9

and many other titles. It might well be asked, furthermore, how an influence or impersonal power can be grieved (Eph. 4:30), or quenched (1 Thess. 5:19); or how can an attribute convict, guide, or speak (Acts 13:2)?

## THE IMMORTALITY OF THE SOUL

The immortality of the human soul is generally denied by pseudo-Christian cults. Man, it is taught, is subject to a physical death that is the cessation of existence. He does not have the inherent ability to live forever—anywhere. "Don't say," we are told, "that man has a soul. Rather, say 'man *is* a soul.' When he dies, the whole man dies. Body and soul are one, and at death, body and soul enter the condition known as Soul Sleep, a condition of total unconsciousness." It is further taught that those who die in Christ will be resurrected immortal at the second coming of Christ, while those who die in their sins will be raised at the last day to be totally annihilated. There is no eternal hell for the wicked or anyone else.

The Bible teaches that when God created man, he "breathed into his nostrils the breath of life; and man became a living being" (Gen. 2:7). This particular act of God distinguishes man from every other creature. The souls of men are inherently immortal and indestructible, and yet potentially subject to spiritual death because of sin. Spiritual death is eternal separation from God. It is *not* extinction. The body, created from the dust of the earth, is mortal and subject to physical death, which is separation of soul from body. The body dies and returns to the dust. The soul (or spirit) of the believer goes immediately to be with Christ; that of the unbeliever goes to sheol (Old Testament), called hades in the New Testament. That is the place of *immediate* punishment (Luke 16:23).

The apostle Paul wrote that it was better to depart and to be "with Christ, for that is very much better" (Phil. 1:23). Again, he expressed his willingness to be "absent from the body and to be at home with the Lord" (2 Cor. 5:8). There is not the slightest intimation of an unconscious period subsequent to death. In His declaration to Martha, our Lord Jesus Christ refuted her stated belief in a resurrection only at "the last day." "I am the resurrection and the life," Jesus said (John 11:25-26). Resurrection and life are not far-off events; they are ever present for those who believe in Him.

References in the psalms seem to suggest a lesser degree of awareness after death. In Psalm 115:17, for instance, it is written that "the dead do not praise the LORD, nor do any who go down into silence." This appears as man's comparison of relative situations on earth and in sheol. It was written prior to the coming of the One who "brought life and immortality to light through the gospel" (2 Tim. 1:10). "Today you shall be with Me in Paradise" was the promise of the Lord to the penitent thief on the cross. "But that life and consciousness continue between death and resurrection is directly affirmed in Scripture (Isa. 14:9-11; Mt. 22:32; Mk. 9:43-48; Lk. 16:19-31; 2 Cor. 5:6-8; Phil. 1:21; Rev. 6:9-11)."[4]

The annihilation of the wicked dead is nowhere taught in the Bible. The state of the wicked in eternal fire is as clearly stated as is that of the righteous in eternal bliss. In Matthew 25:41 and 46 the Greek word for "eternal" is used in both places, with reference to the punishment of the wicked and with reference to the life of the righteous. In 2 Thessalonians 1:9 the same word is rendered "eternal" with reference to the destruction of the disobedient "from the presence of the Lord." A further point might be made from Revelation 19:20 and 20:10. The beast and the false prophet will be cast into the "lake of fire" at the Battle of Armageddon. One thousand years later they are still in that "lake of fire and brimstone," where they shall be "tormented day and night forever and ever." No cessation of existence, but everlasting destruction.

## THE DOCTRINE OF ESCHATOLOGY

Just a final word about the teaching of the cults concerning the future. Differences will be noted as the cults are individually treated. Usually there is the concept of

4. *The New Scofield Reference Bible* (New York: Oxford, 1967), p. 702.

a millennium, which may or may not be preceded by a
great tribulation. Judgments are prominent, both of the
righteous and unrighteous. Frequently those are separated
by the thousand years of the Millennium, and are associated with the first and second resurrections. Annihilation
of the wicked is the common teaching, with "eternal life"
for the faithful. This eternal life is variously portrayed as
being on the cleansed and renewed earth, or on another
sphere somewhere in the heavens.

# 1

## Mormonism

THE CHURCH OF JESUS CHRIST OF LATTER-DAY SAINTS (whose members have been nicknamed Mormons) claims to be the restoration of the true church established by Jesus Christ. It has no association in any way with Roman Catholicism or with Protestantism. "Its theology, its organization, and its practices are in many respects entirely unique among today's Christian denominations."[1] "It possesses the divine priesthood of God, . . . and is headed by prophets and Apostles as was the Church in the days of Peter and Paul."[2] Indeed, "if it had not been for Joseph Smith and the restoration, there would be no salvation. There is no salvation outside The Church of Jesus Christ of Latter-day Saints."[3]

In numerous publications it is emphasized that the church which had been established by Jesus Christ became corrupt. Apostasy triumphed and divinely appointed authority ceased. The church "drifted without direction" after the death of the apostle John. There was no revelation, authority, or divinely approved ministry until the true church was restored through the prophet Joseph Smith.

Born in Sharon, Vermont, in 1805, Smith had moved to Palmyra, New York. There, in 1820, he reported seeing

1. Gordon B. Hinckley, *What of the Mormons?* (Salt Lake City: Deseret News Press, n.d.), p. 2.
2. Mark E. Peterson, *Which Church Is Right?* (Salt Lake City: Deseret News Press, n.d.), p. 25.
3. Bruce R. McConkie, *Mormon Doctrine* (Bookcraft, Salt Lake City, 1966), p. 670 (hereafter cited as McConkie).

his first heavenly vision. Two personages appeared. Their "brightness and glory defy all description. . . . One of them spake unto me, calling me by name and said, pointing to the other—*This is My Beloved Son. Hear Him!*"[4]

There followed a series of visitations from a "resurrected personage" named Moroni. These visitations culminated on Sept. 22, 1827. Moroni delivered to Smith the "golden plates," the translation of which is known as the Book of Mormon. In May 1829, John the Baptist appeared and ordained Smith along with Oliver Cowdery to the Aaronic priesthood. In June of that same year, Peter, James, and John "came to Joseph Smith and Oliver Cowdery and conferred upon them the Melchizedek Priesthood" (McConkie 478). This established the authority of the "Church," for without the "Melchizedek Priesthood" "salvation in the kingdom of God" is not "available for men on earth" (McConkie 479).

On April 6, 1830, The Church of Jesus Christ of Latter-day Saints was formally established in Fayette, New York, with six members. It has grown to a present membership of more than three million, with branches in every state of the Union and more than a score of foreign lands. Various estimates cite as many as fourteen thousand missionaries in active ministry, with some six thousand serving part-time. Full-time missionaries serve voluntarily, without pay, normally for a period of two years. The majority are young men between the ages of nineteen and twenty-five.

4. P Joseph Smith 2:17. The Mormon sacred books are cited in the following ways in this book: The Book of Mormon and the Pearl of Great Price are each composed of individual books, the same basic format as is found in the Bible. References to the individual books begin either with the abbreviation BM (for the Book of Mormon) or with P (for the Pearl of Great Price) and are followed by the title of the individual book, the chapter number, and the verse number—BM 2 Nephi 29:6 and P Joseph Smith 2:35, for example. Doctrine and Covenants is divided into sections. References to individual sections begin with the abbreviation D&C, which is followed by the section number and the verse number—D&C 27:1, for example. The three books are published by The Church of Jesus Christ of Latter-day Saints at Salt Lake City, Utah.

## THE SOURCES OF AUTHORITY

We believe the Bible to be the word of God as far as it is translated correctly; we also believe the Book of Mormon to be the word of God.

We believe all that God has revealed, all that He does now reveal, and we believe that He will yet reveal many great and important things pertaining to the Kingdom of God [P Articles of Faith 8-9].

It is strongly emphasized that the canon of Scripture has never been closed. God's direction has always been by personal communication through commissioned servants. God's laws in one period have been repealed in others, "when a more advanced stage of the divine plan had been reached."[5] Thus in the Sermon on the Mount (see Matt. 5:17-18), the Savior, it is taught, repealed the Law of Moses. Current and continued revelations are held to be essential characteristics of the church in order that the officers might teach with authority. The president of the church, in particular, is "like unto Moses—"a seer, a revelator, a translator, and a prophet, having all the gifts of God which he bestows upon the head of the church" (D&C 107:91-92). He speaks, upon occasion, with as much authority as does the Bible, or as any other of the accepted sacred books, the Book of Mormon, the Doctrine and Covenants, and the Pearl of Great Price.

A. The official version of the Bible used by the Mormon Church is the King James Version. A revision by Joseph Smith, called the Inspired Version, was not completed and is not used by the Salt Lake City group. It should be noted that to the Mormon the Bible is not absolute in authority, and neither final nor complete in its revelation. The qualifying clause "as far as it is translated correctly" suggests

5. James E. Talmage, *A Study of the Articles of Faith* (Salt Lake City: The Church of Jesus Christ of Latter-day Saints, 1961), p. 303 (hereafter cited as Talmage).

errors in translation which presumably have been corrected by subsequent revelations.

B. The Book of Mormon "is a divinely inspired record, made by the prophets of the ancient peoples who inhabited the American continent for centuries before and after the time of Christ" (Talmage 255). It "contains a record of . . . the fulness of the gospel" (D&C 20:9; see also 42:12, etc.). The prophet himself declared that "the Book of Mormon was the most correct of any book on earth, and the keystone of our religion" (McConkie 99, quoting Joseph Smith).

It tells the epic story of two waves of immigration to the American continent. In the first, the Jaredite nation "followed their leader from the Tower of Babel at the time of the confusion of tongues" (Talmage 260) about 2,250 B.C. These people flourished until 590 B.C., when internal warfare led to their total destruction. The final battle took place at the hill Cumorah, near the present Palmyra, New York. The second migration was under Lehi, of the tribe of Manasseh, about the year 600 B.C. Two nations, the Nephite and the Lamanite, came from Lehi's sons Nephi and Laman. The former "advanced in the arts of civilization, built large cities, and established prosperous commonwealths" (Talmage 260). The latter "fell under the curse of divine displeasure; they became dark in skin . . . and degenerated into the fallen state in which the American Indians—their lineal descendants—were found . . . in later times" (Talmage 260). The final struggle between these two nations also ended at Cumorah, about A.D. 421. The last Nephite survivor, Moroni, completed the Book of Mormon on the golden plates and hid them in the hill Cumorah. He later appeared, a resurrected being, in 1823-27 and gave the plates to Joseph Smith for translation.

The plates were inscribed in characters called "reformed Egyptian" (BM Mormon 9:32). To enable translation,

Smith was given the "Urim and Thummim." Perhaps resembling a pair of eyeglasses, these were "two stones in silver bows—and these stones [were] fastened to a breastplate" (P Joseph Smith 2:35). With the aid of these, he completed the translation between December 1827 and February 1828. The story is told in the "Writings of Joseph Smith," which is found in the Pearl of Great Price. In "Writings of Joseph Smith" 2:63-65, Smith cited Professor Charles Anthon as certifying the authenticity of the "reformed Egyptian characters." Anthon vehemently denied this, branding the whole story as "perfectly false." In published statements, the Smithsonian Institution denied knowledge of any authentic cases of ancient Hebrew or Egyptian writing having been found in the New World.[6]

Nevertheless, it is declared that "almost all of the doctrines of the gospel are taught in the Book of Mormon with much greater clarity and perfection than . . . in the Bible. Anyone . . . will find conclusive proof of the superiority of the Book of Mormon teachings" (McConkie 99).

Apparently, Mormon missionaries make much of the claim that the prophet Ezekiel spoke of two books, using the imagery of "two sticks" (Ezek. 37:16-17). The Bible, they say, is the stick of Judah. The Book of Mormon is the stick of Ephraim and records God's dealings with a portion of the tribe of Joseph. It is "now in the hands of church members who nearly all are of Ephraim" (McConkie 767; see also D&C 27:5).

In truth, the word translated "stick" literally means "tree, wood, or pole." The "stick" is the emblem of the royal scepter. Thus it is that the "stick of Judah" represents the Southern Kingdom; the "stick of Joseph" is the Northern Kingdom, of which the first king was Jeroboam, of the

---

6. For further details concerning the genuineness of the Book of Mormon, see Gordon R. Lewis, *Confronting the Cults* (Nutley, N.J.: Presby & Ref., 1966), pp. 52 ff.

tribe of Ephraim. Ezekiel the prophet was predicting the
restoration and future union of the two kingdoms.

C. Doctrine and Covenants is composed of 136 sections,
of which all but two are "revelations given to Joseph Smith,
the Prophet" (title page). Section 135 tells of his martyr-
dom, and 136 is "The Word and Will of the Lord, given
through President Brigham Young." An official declaration
prohibiting polygamy was appended in 1890 by President
Wilford Woodruff.

Significant revelations in this book pertain to baptism
for the dead (sections 124, 127-28), celestial marriage (section 132:19c-20), and plural marriage (section 132).
In contrast, 42:22-23 and 49:15-16 seem to command mo-
nogamy! The Book of Mormon says nothing about the first
two matters, and strongly denounces polygamy (Jacob 2:
23-36).

D. The Pearl of Great Price is a small volume containing "a selection from the revelations, translations, and nar-
rations of Joseph Smith" (title page). It is usually bound
with the Doctrine and Covenants. The Thirteen Articles of
Faith are also included.

### The Doctrine of God

"We believe in God the Eternal Father, and in His Son
Jesus Christ, and in the Holy Ghost" (P Articles of Faith,
1).

The Book of Mormon seems to equate the Mormon concept of the Trinity with that of orthodox Christianity:
"This is the doctrine of Christ, and the only and true doctrine of the Father, and of the Son, and of the Holy Ghost,
which is one God, without end" (BM 2 Nephi 31:21; see
also Alma 11:44, etc.). The theologian Talmage, however,
explains that "three personages composing the great pre-
siding council of the universe have revealed themselves to
man. . . . These three are separate individuals, physically

distinct from each other" (Talmage 39). Refuting the *Westminster Shorter Catechism*, which states that "there are three persons in the Godhead; the Father, the Son, and the Holy Ghost; and these three are one God, the same in substance, equal in power and glory" (Question 6), Talmage declares that this "cannot rationally be construed to mean that the Father, the Son, and the Holy Ghost are one in substance and in person" (Talmage 40). The oneness of the Godhead, it is declared, "implies no mystical union of substance, nor any unnatural and therefore impossible blending of personality" (Talmage 41). McConkie puts it plainly: "There are three *Gods* . . . separate in personality, . . . united as one in purpose, in plan, and in all the attributes of perfection" (McConkie 317). The plural word *Elohim* is used as the exalted name, the title of God, the Eternal Father.

A. God is "an organized being just as we are, who are now in the flesh."[7] This is in keeping with the doctrine that God is a "progressive being, . . . his perfection possesses . . . the capacity of eternal increase" (Talmage 529). He "was perhaps once a child, and mortal like we ourselves, and rose step by step in the scale of progress."[8] Involved in the scheme of eternal progression, He is simply far, far ahead of us, His children. It is reiterated that "as man is, God once was; as God is, man may become."[9] Thus it is taught that Abraham and Isaac and Jacob "have entered into their exaltation and are not angels, but are gods" (D&C 132:37). It remained for Brigham Young to confuse things somewhat by adding, "Adam is our father and god, the only God with whom we have to do."[10]

7. Joseph F. Smith, *Gospel Doctrine* (Salt Lake City: Deseret Book Co., 1963), p. 64.
8. Orson Hyde, in Brigham Young, *Journal of Discourses* (Liverpool, 1854-75), 1:123.
9. Lorenzo Snow, quoted in Anthony A. Hoekema, *The Four Major Cults* (Grand Rapids: Eerdmans, 1963), p. 39.
10. Brigham Young, in *Journal of Discourses*, 1:50.

B. "The Father has a body of flesh and bones as tangible as man's" (D&C 130:22). This is stressed in the Mormon handbook for missionaries as part of the revelation given to Joseph Smith. He saw two personages "of flesh and bones."[11] Thus it is taught that to "deny the materiality of God's person is to deny God; ... an immaterial body cannot exist" (Talmage 48). (In contrast, note Luke 24: 36-43; John 4:24; 1 Tim. 1:17; 6:16. Also see "D." below—the Holy Spirit.)

C. God is omnipresent. But "this does not mean that the actual person of any one member of the Godhead can be physically present in more than one place at one time" (Talmage 43). Since it is held that "personality" implies "materiality," it must be accepted that "God possesses a form . . . of definite proportions and therefore of limited extension in space" (Talmage 43). His senses and powers, however, are infinite, including that of transferring Himself from place to place. He is likewise omniscient and omnipotent "through the agency of angels and ministering servants," and is thus "in continuous communication with all parts of creation" (Talmage 44).

D. The Holy Spirit is "a personage of Spirit" (D&C 130: 22). He does not have a body of flesh and bones, like the Father and the Son. He is described as "the influence of Deity, the light of Christ, or of Truth, which proceeds forth from the presence of God to fill the immensity of space, and to quicken the understanding of men."[12] Nevertheless, He "can be in only one place at one time" (McConkie 359), although He "emanates from Deity" like "electricity, . . . which fills the earth and the air, and is everywhere present" (McConkie 753).

E. There are many Gods. The following excerpt from McConkie's *Mormon Doctrine* is explicit:

11. *Uniform System for Teaching Investigators* (Salt Lake City: Deseret News Press), p. 31.
12. Smith, *Gospel Doctrine*, p. 60.

"*Every man who reigns in celestial glory is a god to his dominions,*" the Prophet said. (*Teachings,* p. 374.) Hence, the Father, who shall continue to all eternity as the God of exalted beings, is a *God of Gods.* Further, as the Prophet also taught, there is "*a God above the Father of our Lord Jesus Christ.* . . . If Jesus Christ was the Son of God, and John discovered that *God the Father of Jesus Christ had a Father,* you may suppose that he had a Father also. Where was there ever a son without a father? . . . Hence if Jesus had a Father, can we not believe that *he* had a Father also?" (*Teachings,* pp. 370, 373.) In this way both the Father and the Son, as also all exalted beings, are now or in due course will become Gods of Gods. (*Teachings,* pp. 342-376.) [McConkie 322-23]

Related to this is the declaration that "Abraham and Isaac and Jacob have entered into their exaltation, and are not angels, but are gods" (D&C 132:37). In keeping with the grand scheme of eternal progression, "there never was a time when there were not Gods and worlds, and when men were not passing through the same ordeals that we are now passing through."[13]

F. The Gods have wives! There is a Mother in Heaven! This is normal teaching related to the fact that God is *literally* the father of our spirits. (See "The Doctrine of Man" below.) "Each god, through his wife or wives, raises up a numerous family of sons and daughters."[14] "The begetting of children makes a man a father and a woman a mother whether we are dealing with man in his mortal or immortal state" (McConkie 516). God, the exalted and glorified Man of Holiness, "could not be a Father unless a Woman of like glory, perfection, and holiness was associated with him as a Mother" (McConkie 516). This "glori-

13. Brigham Young, in John A. Widtsoe, ed., *Discourses of Brigham Young* (Salt Lake City: Deseret Book Co., 1954), p. 22.
14. Orson Pratt, *The Seer* 1, no. 3 (March 1853):37.

ous truth of celestial parentage" (McConkie 516) is expressed in a Latter-day Saint hymn:

> In the heavens are parents single?
> No; the thought makes reason stare!
> Truth is reason, truth eternal,
> Tells me I've a Mother there [In McConkie 517].

Following his statement that Adam is the Mormons' God, Brigham Young declared that Adam "brought Eve, one of his wives, with him."[15] In the same way, mortal beings who gain the ultimate exaltation will become eternal fathers and mothers, and will populate their own worlds with their own spirit children. This involves celestial marriage, the rite by which participants continue on as husband and wife in the celestial kingdom (see "THE DOCTRINE OF THE ATONEMENT" below).

## THE DOCTRINE OF JESUS CHRIST

Jesus Christ "is the eternal Jehovah, the promised Messiah, Redeemer and Savior, the Way, the Truth, and the Life" (McConkie 129). Although it may seem to be in keeping with Bible teaching, Mormonism's Christology is nevertheless not that of orthodox Christianity.

A. "Among the spirit children of Elohim, the first-born was and is Jehovah, or Jesus Christ, to whom all others are juniors."[16] This distinction as "first-born" describes Christ's relationship to *all* God's children. Angels and demons, as well as human beings, are included. Various types of beings serve God as angels, or messengers. *All* were the children of the Father. "The devil . . . is a spirit son of God who was born in the morning of pre-existence" (McConkie 192). Devils, or demons, "are the spirit beings who followed Lucifer in his war of rebellion in preexistence" (McConkie 195). One-third of the spirit children of God fol-

15. Brigham Young, in *Journal of Discourses*, 1:50.
16. Smith, *Gospel Doctrine*, p. 70.

lowed Lucifer in that rebellion. The difference between Christ and man or demon is therefore one of degree, or of position, and not of kind. This rejects any thought of His distinctive deity.

B. "By obedience and devotion to the truth he attained that pinnacle of intelligence which ranked him as a God ... while yet in his pre-existent state" (McConkie 129). It should be noted that this is not the normal pattern. Birth in a mortal body is deemed necessary for the ultimate attainment of godhood. See "THE DOCTRINE OF GOD," sec. A.)

C. Jesus Christ was the executive of the Father in the work of creation. In this work He was aided by Michael (or Adam), "Enoch, Noah, Abraham, Moses, Peter, James, and John, Joseph Smith and many others" (McConkie 169).

D. He was born of the virgin Mary. This assures His *unique* status. It is emphasized, however, that although the conception took place by the power of the Holy Ghost, Christ is not the Son of the Holy Ghost, but of the Father. Talmage adds: "Elohim is LITERALLY the Father of the Spirit of Jesus Christ, and also of the body" (Talmage 466). "He was not born without the aid of a man, and that man was God."[17] Brigham Young adds: "Who is the Father? He is the first of the human family; ... the same character that was in the garden of Eden, and who is our Father in Heaven."[18]

E. He was altogether sinless. "He is essentially greater than any and all others, by reason (1) of His seniority as the oldest or firstborn; (2) of His unique status in the flesh as the offspring of a mortal mother and of an immortal, or resurrected and glorified, Father; (3) of His selection and foreordination as the one and only Redeemer and

17. Joseph F. Smith, *Doctrines of Salvation* (Salt Lake City: Bookcraft, 1956), 1:18.
18. Brigham Young, in *Journal of Discourses,* 1:50-51.

Savior of the race; and (4) of His transcendent sinlessness"
(Talmage 472).

F. He died on the cross, voluntarily and willingly giving His life for the redemption of mankind. (See "THE
DOCTRINE OF THE ATONEMENT.")

G. He rose again the third day, with a tangible body of
flesh and bones. In addition to the resurrection appearances as recorded in the Bible, the Book of Mormon tells
of His coming to the Americas as a resurrected being. He
organized the church among the Nephite people, with
twelve disciples to lead it (BM 3 Nephi 11).

H. He is coming again in power and great glory to set
up His kingdom on earth (see "THE DOCTRINE OF LAST
THINGS [ESCHATOLOGY]").

### THE DOCTRINE OF MAN

Life began for man and for all created things (animals,
fowls, fishes, and every living creature—even the earth itself) at the time of their respective spirit creations. However, it must be understood that God did not create anything, in the sense of bringing into primal existence. He
"organized" the elements which are "co-eternal with Him"
(McConkie 751). The elements thus "organized" are
known as "intelligences," or "spirit children" (McConkie
751).

Note: In the broad sweep of eternity, man's advance in
the scheme of eternal progression involves at least four
stages: (1) the premortal or spirit existence, with bodies
"made of a more pure and refined substance than the elements from which mortal bodies are made. (Ether 3:16;
D&C 131:7-8.)" (McConkie 589). (2) Mortal life on earth,
with body and spirit temporarily joined together (D&C 93:
33). (3) In the spirit world, the abiding place of disem-
bodied spirits, after death. It is "upon this earth," and will
be "without inhabitants" after the resurrection (McConkie

762). (4) Immortality, the resurrected state with body and spirit *inseparably* connected.

A. The spirit children of God were given the right of free agency—that is, the freedom to choose good or evil. Their choices determined to a degree their later state. One-third rebelled along with Satan, and fell with him. They will remain "unembodied," never to enter the scheme of eternal progression (see "THE DOCTRINE OF ETERNITY [THE FINAL STATE]," sec. D). Two-thirds stood "affirmatively for Christ," but some were less "valiant" than others. This explains the "millions of insane and afflicted people upon the earth," and "those living in squalor, filth, poverty, and degradation."[19] What they are is the result of choices made in premortal existence. For the same reason, Blacks who are of the lineage of Cain, have been, until 1978, denied the priesthood and its attendant blessings in this mortal state (see addendum, "THE MORMON BLACK AND THE PRIESTHOOD").

B. In the premortal state, Adam was Michael, the archangel (D&C 27:11; 107:54). As the first man, he was formed "in the image of his spiritual Father, God" (Talmage 63). He was placed with one of his preincarnate wives, Eve, in the Garden of Eden. This place, also called Adam-ondi-Ahman, is located in "an area for which Jackson County, Missouri, is the center" (McConkie 20). Zion, the New Jerusalem, will be built there in the latter days.

C. "Adam fell that men might be; and men are, that they might have joy" (BM 2 Nephi 2:25). Adam and Eve had immortal bodies. Eve, however, sinned and became mortal. That created a dilemma for Adam. He had been given two commands: first, multiply and replenish the earth; second, do not touch the forbidden tree. Eve was now mortal. Adam, being yet immortal, could not obey

19. John J. Stewart, *Mormonism and the Negro* (Orem, Utah: Bookmark, 1967), pp. 29-30.

the first command without disobeying the second! "He deliberately and wisely chose to stand by the first and greater commandment, and . . . partook of the fruit" (Talmage 65).

The Fall was foreordained within the purpose of God. It is to be regarded as a good thing in that it was a means of providing billions of preexistent spirits with mortal tabernacles. Adam cried, "Blessed be the name of God, for because of my transgression my eyes are opened, and in this life I shall have joy" (P Moses 5:10). Eve exults, "Were it not for our transgression we never should have had seed, and never should have known good and evil, and the joy of our redemption, and the eternal life which God giveth unto all the obedient" (P Moses 5:11). The Mormon catechism declares that the Fall should be thought of as one of the great advancements toward eternal exaltation and happiness. Man thus became mortal, a blessing in disguise in that it provided the opportunity for eternal progression and perfection to all spirit children of Elohim. It also brought to man the knowledge of good and evil. This "is an essential element in the commission of sin, and our first parents did not have this knowledge until after they had partaken of the fruit" (McConkie 804).

D. The doctrine of original sin is denied by the second article of faith: "We believe that men will be punished for their own sins, and not for Adam's transgression" (P Articles of Faith 2). "Every spirit of man was innocent in the beginning" (D&C 93:38). The age of accountability is reckoned to be eight, since it is stated that "their children shall be baptized for the remission of their sins when eight years old" (D&C 68:27).

### THE DOCTRINE OF THE ATONEMENT

We believe that through the Atonement of Christ, all

mankind may be saved, by obedience to the laws and ordinances of the gospel.

We believe that the first principles and ordinances of
the gospel are: first, Faith in the Lord Jesus Christ; second, Repentance; third, Baptism by immersion for the remission of sins; fourth, Laying on of hands for the gift of
the Holy Ghost [P Articles of Faith 3-4].

In contrast to Lucifer's plan, which would have com-
pelled men to obey God, Christ offered Himself so that
men might be free to choose for themselves. There are two
aspects of salvation: general, or unconditional; and individual, or conditional.

A. General, or unconditional, salvation is assured for all.
Bodily weakness, disease, and physical death came upon
all men because of the transgression of Adam. Men become *mortal* (which means that they become subject to
"separation of the eternal spirit from the mortal body"
(McConkie 185). Christ, by the work of redemption,
overcame physical death and *guaranteed* physical resurrection to all living things. This *is* immortality! "Even the
unbeliever, the heathen, and the child who dies before
reaching the years of discretion, all are redeemed by the
Saviour's self-sacrifice from the individual consequences
of the Fall. . . . The resurrection of the body is one of the
victories achieved by Christ through His atoning sacrifice"
(Talmage 85). Included also are "beasts, the fowls of the
air, and the fishes of the sea" (D&C 29:23-25), and "the
earth . . . and the infinite expanse of the worlds in immensity" (McConkie 642). The only exceptions are the sons
of perdition.

B. Individual, or conditional, salvation pertains to the
eternal progression of the individual soul and is entirely
contingent upon obedience, works, and choices in *this*
sphere of existence. The guarantee of immortality (physi-

cal resurrection) is not synonymous with "eternal life," or "exaltation." It does not assure "godhood" in eternity.

There are three possible spheres of existence in eternity. Only one, the celestial, is the abode of those who continue in the eternal progression to be as "gods." (See "THE DOCTRINE OF ETERNITY [THE FINAL STATE]" below.) Entrance to this sphere is on the basis of obedience to the laws and ordinances, and "by devotion and faithfulness, by enduring to the end in righteousness and obedience, it is then possible to merit a celestial reward" (McConkie 116; see also D&C 20:29; BM 2 Nephi 9:23-24). It is with this in mind that Talmage asserts that "the sectarian dogma of justification by faith alone has exercised an influence for evil" (Talmage 479). Where one goes after he is resurrected is determined by his individual responses, actions, and choices *now*.

C. "To the Mormons, baptism . . . is the most vital and significant of all ordinances—the very gateway into the kingdom of heaven—an indispensable step in our salvation and exaltation."[20] Without it, forgiveness of sins is impossible. As Joseph Smith stated, "They who believe not on your words, and are not baptized in water in my [Jesus'] name, for the remission of their sins, that they may receive the Holy Ghost, shall be damned" (D&C 84:74). Infant baptism is considered a "gross perversion" of true Christian doctrine.

Baptism for the dead is the "welding link" between "fathers and children" (D&C 128:18). This unique practice occupies a prominent place in current Mormon temple activity, and presumably will be the great work during the Millennium. The basic teaching is that many have died without the opportunity to hear and believe the gospel. To them, in the spirit-world, Christ went and preached

20. Wallace F. Bennett, *Why I Am a Mormon* (Boston: Beacon Press, 1958), p. 124.

after His death. First Corinthians 15:29 and 1 Peter 3:18-22 are claimed as supporting this. There are others "who have gone into the spirit world who have never submitted to the ordinance of baptism, while vast numbers of those who have been baptized had the ordinance administered by one who held no rightful authority whatever."[21] They also are given opportunity to hear and to believe. But even spirit believers cannot be saved without water baptism. Therefore baptism by proxy is a major activity for which

> the Latter-day Saints are assiduously engaged in erecting temples wherein this ordinance may be performed. . . . The Saints are flocking to the temples of the Lord and redeeming their dead from the grasp of Satan. They are performing a great and mighty work for the human family who have lived upon the earth in the different ages of the world's history, and who, in some instances, by revelation, make manifest to their children or friends the fact that they have accepted the Gospel in the spirit world.[22]

In pursuit of this activity, the "Church has accumulated more than 150,000 rolls of microfilm covering more than 230 million pages of vital statistics, and the work is still going on."[23] There were said to have been 3,607,962 such baptisms during 1965.

D. "Celestial marriage is the gate to an exaltation in the highest heaven within the celestial world" (McConkie 118; see also D&C 131:1-4). This rite is performed only in Mormon temples. By it the man and woman are "sealed for time and eternity" and "have eternal claim on their posterity, and the gift of eternal increase."[24] Provided they keep all the other terms and conditions set forth, they be-

---

21. John Morgan, *The Plan of Salvation* (Salt Lake City: Deseret News Press, n.d.), p. 22.
22. Ibid., p. 23.
23. Bennett, p. 130.
24. Smith, *Doctrines of Salvation*, 2:44.

come "gods in their own right" (McConkie 118). This exalting ordinance can also be performed vicariously, for the benefit of worthy dead.

### THE DOCTRINE OF LAST THINGS (ESCHATOLOGY)

We believe in the literal gathering of Israel and in the restoration of the Ten Tribes; that Zion will be built upon this [the American] continent; that Christ will reign personally upon the earth; and that the earth will be renewed and receive its paradisiacal glory [P Articles of Faith 10].

A. The gatherings are three in number: "the house of Joseph will be established in America, the house of Judah in Palestine, and . . . the Lost Tribes will come to Ephraim in America to receive their blessings in due course" (McConkie 306; from D&C 133).

1. The people of Israel will assemble in the land of Zion, which is the North American continent. It is pointed out that upon Ephraim, the son of Joseph, was conferred the birthright in Israel (Gen. 48:5-22). The Northern Kingdom of Israel, later scattered over all the known world, was frequently referred to as Ephraim. Thus Ephraim "stands at head in the Latter days . . . and must be gathered first to prepare the way . . . for the rest of the tribes of Israel."[25] Further, "Joseph Smith was pure Ephraimite,"[26] of the lineage of Joseph, and "the great majority of those who have come into the Church are Ephraimites."[27] Thus the House of Israel is being gathered as men and women join The Church of Jesus Christ of Latter-day Saints, and the house of Israel is being established in Zion.

2. The house of Judah (the Jewish people) are now being gathered to Jerusalsm, mostly in unbelief. "The great body of [them] will not receive Christ as their Redeemer

25. Smith, *Doctrines of Salvation,* 3:252.
26. Ibid., p. 253.
27. Ibid., p. 252.

until he comes himself and makes himself manifest unto them."[28]

3. The lost ten tribes are descendants of people carried away captive by Shalmaneser of Assyria (721 B.C.). Many are still living in "the north countries," where the Lord has hidden them. Proof of their existence is found in the Book of Mormon (BM 3 Nephi 16:1-4; 17:4). They were visited by the resurrected Lord after his ministry on this continent among the Nephites. "In due course [they] will return and come to the children of Ephraim to receive their blessings. This great gathering will take place under the direction of the President of The Church of Jesus Christ of Latter-day Saints" (McConkie 458).

B. The millennial reign of Christ will follow the gathering of Israel and establishment of an earthly Zion.

1. The first resurrection will inaugurate this glorious period of peace and prosperity. Called the "resurrection of life," or "of the just," it will be in two parts. Those being resurrected with celestial bodies will come forth in the morning of the first resurrection. They will be caught up to meet the Lord, and will descend with Him, to reign together with Him (D&C 88:95-98). Apparently included are all children who die before reaching the age of accountability. In the afternoon, those with "terrestrial bodies" will rise (see "THE DOCTRINE OF ETERNITY [THE FINAL STATE]," sec. B). They live on the earth during the millennial reign.

2. The second coming of Christ will be marked by destruction of the wicked. This event will occur at the end of the Battle of Armageddon, which will then be in progress. The earth will be cleansed of all its corruption and wickedness. All the wicked, not worthy of either celestial or terrestrial glory, will spend the thousand years in "the prison house prepared for them." There they are to "re-

28. Ibid., p. 9.

pent and cleanse themselves through the things which they shall suffer."[29]

3. The earth will be cleansed by fire, renewed, and given its paradisiacal glory, a return to the "edenic, terrestrial state."

4. Satan will be bound, his powers limited for the 1,000 years. Men will be to a degree relieved from temptation, but "sin will not be wholly abolished, nor will death be banished" (Talmage 371). "Children will live to reach maturity in the flesh, and then may be changed to a condition of immortality" (Talmage 371).

5. "Mortal and immortal beings will tenant the earth, and communion with heavenly powers will be common" (Talmage 371).

6. The great work of the Millennium will be the vicarious performing of "saving and exalting ordinances" (baptism and celestial marriage) on behalf of "worthy dead who did not have opportunity during life" (McConkie 501).

7. The gospel will be taught with great power, and "eventually all people will embrace the truth."[30]

8. The second resurrection takes place at the end of the Millennium. As in the case of the first resurrection, it has two parts. Those who are destined for telestial glory (see "THE DOCTRINE OF ETERNITY [THE FINAL STATE]," sec. C are raised in the "fore part." In the "latter end" comes the resurrection of damnation, pertaining to the sons of perdition.

9. Satan will be released, and will lead the final rebellion at the end of the Millennium. He will deceive men again and will gather together "his armies, even the hosts of hell" (McConkie 501). His defeat will be total. All, including Satan, will be cast into "punishment so terrible

29. Ibid., p. 60.
30. Ibid., p. 64.

that the knowledge is withheld from all except those who are consigned to this doom" (Talmage 60).

C. The earth will die, be resurrected, and become "a celestialized body fit for the abode of the most exalted intelligences" (Talmage 375). "The Millennium, with all its splendor, is but a more advanced stage of preparation, by which the earth and its inhabitants will approach foreordained perfection" (Talmage 375).

### THE DOCTRINE OF ETERNITY (THE FINAL STATE)

There are three eternal kingdoms of widely differing glories, and another place for the sons of perdition. The status and place of the individual in eternity is the outcome of his own efforts, and "not Christ's sacrifice."[31] Each kingdom is organized on a plan of gradation. Advancement within each is possible, but progress from one to another lacks "positive affirmation" (Talmage 409).

A. The celestial kingdom (the sphere of exaltation) will be located on the "resurrected" earth. It will be the abode of those who have been cleansed of sins and have continued obedient to the laws and ordinances of the gospel. "They shall be gods, because they have no end" (D&C 132: 16-26). "They have eternal increase . . . ; that is, they have spirit children in the resurrection, in relation to which offspring they stand in the same position that God our Father stands to us" (McConkie 257). All who attain unto this sphere shall dwell in the presence of God and His Christ forever (D&C 76:62).

B. The terrestrial kingdom will be peopled by those who did not accept the gospel until they were in the spirit world. With them will be "accountable persons who die without law; . . . honorable men of the earth who are blinded . . . and who therefore do not accept and live the gospel law" (McConkie 784); and members of The Church

31. Bennett, p. 191.

of Jesus Christ of Latter-day Saints who were not valiant, but were lukewarm. They remain unmarried and without exaltation; and they receive the presence of the Son, but not the fullness of the Father.

C. The telestial kingdom is the place to which "most of the adult people who have lived from the day of Adam . . . will go" (McConkie 778). Joseph Smith saw in a vision that the inhabitants of the telestial world "were as innumerable as the stars in the firmament of heaven, or as the sand upon the seashore" (D&C 76:109). Having rejected Christ and lived wickedly, they will be the last to be resurrected, and they will have suffered the wrath of God in the spirit world. In this sphere they will never know the presence of God or of Christ, but shall continue as servants of God.

D. *Perdition* signifies that there is no hope of any degree of salvation. "Two persons, Cain and Satan, have received the title *Perdition*" (McConkie 566). The sons of perdition include the angels who rebelled with Satan, and men who commit unpardonable sin—that is, "having received the testimony of Christ, and having been endowed by the Holy Spirit, [they] then deny the same and defy the power of God" (Talmage 410). The unpardonable sin "can be committed by those only who have received knowledge and conviction of the truth" (Talmage 410). They are doomed to everlasting fire.

However, this is softened by the idea that "there must be an end to future punishment." It is called "eternal punishment" because God is "eternal." "Eternal punishment" is simply "God's punishment; . . . it is the name of the punishment God inflicts, he being eternal in his nature." God has the power to pardon beyond the grave! Eternal punishment may endure "one hour, one day, one week, one year, or an age."[32]

32. Morgan, pp. 23-24.

## POLYGAMY

The practice of polygamy, or plural marriage, "was established as a result of direct revelation, and many of those who followed the same felt they were divinely commanded to do so" (Talmage 424). The record is found in the *Doctrine and Covenants*, section 132. Its heading reads: "Revelation given through Joseph Smith the Prophet at Nauvoo, Illinois, recorded July 12, 1843, relating to the new and everlasting covenant, including the eternity of the marriage covenant, as also plurality of wives." In this revelation it is clear that one of the "essentials for the attainment of the status of godhood" is "marriage duly authorized" (D&C 132). In verses 52 to 54 of section 132, Emma Smith, Joseph's wife, is told that she must prepare to receive additional wives "given" to her husband, otherwise she would be destroyed.

It has been noted that the gods of Mormonism are polygamous, and are constantly begetting children. The second president, Brigham Young, is credited with the statement that "when our father Adam came into the Garden of Eden, . . . he brought Eve, *one of his wives,* with him."[33] Thus it is that the concept that Jesus Christ was married and that he was a polygamist, evokes no consternation. Only by begetting children could he attain unto the utmost in the celestial kingdom.

Polygamy became a controversial issue in later Mormon history. But there is no doubt that the practice was common and that it began with Joseph Smith the Prophet. The sixth president of the church, Joseph F. Smith, wrote: "I can positively state, on indisputable evidence, that Joseph Smith was the author, under God, of the revelation on plural marriage."[34] He cites an affidavit concerning one plural wife of Joseph Smith. He also gives the names of

33. Brigham Young, in *Journal of Discourses*, 1:50.
34. Smith, *Gospel Doctrine*, p. 489.

six other women who testified, under oath, "that they were
sealed during his lifetime to the Prophet Joseph Smith."[35]
Polygamy continued as a church observance in Utah for
ten years without any law being enacted in opposition to
it. Beginning with 1862, however, federal statutes were
framed declaring the practice unlawful. After many ap-
peals by the church had been unsuccessful, Mormon president Wilford Woodruff, the only man on earth holding the
keys of sealing ordinances, issued an official declaration
in 1890. Thereupon the church discontinued the practice
of plural marriage, according to James E. Talmage, one
of the twelve apostles of the Mormon Church (Talmage
424, 524-25).

### THE MORMON BLACK AND THE PRIESTHOOD

As noted above, Joseph Smith was ordained to the
Aaronic priesthood by John the Baptist and to the Melchizedek priesthood by Peter, James, and John. Those
two priesthoods are central in the organization of the Mormons. "As pertaining to eternity, the priesthood is the
eternal power and authority of Deity by which all things
exist; by which they are created, governed, and controlled;
by which the universe and worlds without number have
come rolling into existence; by which the great plan of
creation, redemption, and exaltation operates throughout
immensity. It is the power of God" (McConkie 594).

The lesser priesthood is the Aaronic, containing the
offices of deacon, teacher, priest, and bishop. It is prepara-
tory—by it one is trained for the greater, the Melchizedek
priesthood. This latter has within it the offices of elder,
seventy, high priest, patriarch or evangelist, and apostle.
The Melchizedek priesthood is "the channel through which
all knowledge, doctrine, the plan of salvation, and every

35. Ibid., pp. 489-90.

important matter is revealed from heaven" (McConkie 476). Mormon Doctrine specifically declares "that those spirits sent to earth through the lineage of Cain and of Ham are absolutely denied the priesthood as far as mortal life is concerned" (McConkie 479). The Mormon Church further holds that there were premortal spirits who were "less valiant" than others, and who "thereby had certain spiritual restrictions imposed upon them during mortality." They "are known to us as the *negroes*" (McConkie 527). Blacks are denied the priesthood, and "under no circumstances can they hold this delegation of authority" (McConkie 527). They are "not equal with other races where the receipt of certain spiritual blessings are concerned" (McConkie 527). This is the Lord's doing, and is based on His eternal laws of justice!

It is all the more remarkable that on June 9, 1978, Mormon president Spencer W. Kimball, Prophet, Seer, and Revelator of the Church of Jesus Christ of Latter-day Saints, issued this decree: God "by revelation has confirmed that the long-promised day has come when every faithful, worthy man may receive the holy priesthood, with power to exercise its divine authority. . . . Accordingly, all worthy members of the Church may be ordained to the priesthood without regard for race or color."[36] This long-expected decree was widely promulgated, and was hailed by the fewer than one thousand black members of the church. Apparently no attempt has been made to reconcile these diametrically opposed edicts of "the will and word of the Lord" and His eternal laws of justice. Inasmuch as mortal existence was defined by irreversible actions made in the preexistent spirit world, no doubt explanations are impossible.

36. *Forward Magazine* 2, no. 1 (1978), p. 1. The magazine is published by Christian Research Institute, Box 500, San Juan Capistrano, Calif. 92675.

DIVISIONS IN MORMONISM

At the death of Joseph Smith, a special conference voted on August 8, 1844, at Nauvoo, Illinois, to accept the church council of twelve apostles, headed by Brigham Young, as the interim governing body pending reorganization of a presidency. The main body, numbering some twenty thousand, went with Young to Utah. These composed the beginning of the group usually alluded to when mention is made of "the Mormons." Membership today is approximately two million.

Five dissenting groups refused to follow Brigham Young and formed separate organizations. Of these, only one is significant. It is The Reorganized Church of Jesus Christ of Latter Day Saints, with headquarters at Independence, Missouri. They are called Josephites. The original thousand followed Emma Smith, Joseph's first wife, and were later organized by Joseph Smith, Jr. Today the membership is approximately 175,000. An active publication program emphasizes the differences that exist between themselves and the Utah Mormon Church, as the main body is designated.

Both groups believe in the authenticity of the Book of Mormon. Both accept and publish "many of the revelations given through the Prophet Joseph Smith in our respective versions and additions of the *Doctrine and Covenants*."[37] Differences relate to conflicting views concerning God, the question of polygamy, secret temple rites, and prophetic succession and leadership. Strong exception is taken to the "axiom current among Mormons for many years, 'As man is, God once was; as God is, man may become.' "[38] The teaching that God is Himself a progressive being is rejected. The Reorganized Church teaches that

37. Elbert A. Smith, *Differences That Persist* (Independence, Mo.: Herald Publishing House), p. 6.
38. Ibid., p. 9.

God is eternally unchangeable. With this naturally goes the repudiation of Brigham Young's Adam-God theology. Correlated with this is the denial of the doctrine of celestial marriage as related to the eternal progression and exaltation of men.

The Reorganized Church maintains that polygamy is contrary to the teaching and practice of Joseph Smith. Documental evidence is offered to prove that the accepted story of the plural wives of the Prophet was a deception perpetrated by Brigham Young and his immediate associates. Section 132 of the *Doctrine and Covenants* is not accepted as divine revelation.

In the Kirtland Temple of the Reorganized Church there are no secret meetings of any kind. All meetings are open to the public; none of the sacraments and ordinances is conducted in secret. The "Secret Temple Rites" as practiced by the Mormons of Utah are held to be abhorrent. Finally, the Josephites disavow the claim that Young and his successors are the ordained elders of the church. They followed Joseph Smith, Jr., as the designated successor of his father, and have maintained their own line of "revealed" succession.

This group publishes and uses the Inspired Version of the Bible. Started by Joseph Smith as a revision of the King James Version, it was not completed by him and is therefore not used by the Utah Mormons.

# 2

## Jehovah's Witnesses

JEHOVAH'S WITNESSES are, by their own definition, "servants of Jehovah, the Almighty God, and active witnesses to his sovereign supremacy."[1] Claiming to be followers of "Christ their Leader," they reject any association with the "religious hypocrites of organized Christendom." Anti-Christ is defined as "any organization or individual that is against Christ or Christianity." This includes those who say that "Christ was God incarnate; deny Christ actually came to earth as a Perfect Man of Flesh; the Collective Clergy of Christendom; Pagan Religions; Communistic Red Religion"; and supporters of the United Nations (MS 14-15).

God's sovereignty, they say, was impugned when Adam and Eve rebelled. Therefore the major issue before all heaven and earth is the vindication of the name and sovereignty of Jehovah. *This* is more important than the salvation of men, and will be completely settled at the coming Battle of Armageddon. In the meantime, the faithful members of this organization are demonstrating that there is "a group of persons dedicated to do God's will"[2] and thus are vindicating "his reproached and misrepresented name" (LG 29).

The publication activity of the Jehovah's Witnesses is

1. *Make Sure of All Things* (Brooklyn: Watchtower Bible and Tract Society, 1953), p. 193 (hereafter cited as MS).
2. *Let God Be True* (Brooklyn: Watchtower Bible and Tract Society, 1952), p. 219 (hereafter cited as LG).

simply amazing. The average printing of each issue of *Awake* magazine is 10,125,000 (1977), and the average printing of each issue of *The Watchtower* magazine is 9,200,000 (1978) in 82 languages. The production of cloth-bound books is apparently endless, with considerable repetition of contents. All are written in the same authoritative tone, very convincing to uninformed readers. In vehement and caustic language, particular exception is taken to the orthodox doctrine of the Trinity. The essential deity of Jesus Christ is denied, as is the personality of the Holy Spirit. The efficacy of the atonement is vitiated by the demand for continued faithfulness in witnessing, and any degree of assurance of salvation is virtually impossible. There is unscriptural stress on the 144,000 "followers of Christ" who "only will go to heaven" (MS 196). *They* compose the "body of Christ," and for them are reserved the titles which, in orthodox Christianity, are applied to all true believers. The mass of the Jehovah's Witnesses work incessantly, with the hope of eternity on an earthly paradise. And continuance even there seems contingent upon faithfulness.[3] This "faithfulness in witnessing" is indicated in the reported 307,272,262 hours of witnessing during 1978.

*The organization* known as Jehovah's Witnesses was legally incorporated in 1884 by Charles Taze Russell. It was then known as The Watch Tower Bible and Tract Society. Russell rejected much of the teaching of orthodox Christianity and built his own system of Bible interpretation. His ideas were widely circulated through a seven-volume *Studies in the Scriptures* (Allegheny, Pa.: Watchtower Bible and Tract Society). "It is said that 15 million copies of this series have been distributed."[4] The organiza-

---

3. *From Paradise Lost to Paradise Regained* (Brooklyn: Watchtower Bible and Tract Society, 1958), p. 226.
4. Bruce M. Metzger, *The Jehovah's Witnesses and Jesus Christ* (Princeton, N.J.: Theological Book Agency), p. 65. The booklet is a reprint from *Theology Today* 10, no. 1 (April 1953):65-85.

tion was variously known as Russellites, Millennial Dawn-
ists, Rutherfordites (after Joseph Franklin Rutherford, the
successor to Russell), and International Bible Students.
However, in 1931 the official name became Jehovah's Witnesses. This was based on Isaiah 43:10 (see also 44:8)
which reads: "Ye are my witnesses, saith the Lord [Jeho-
vah]." Rutherford, president since 1917, was succeeded by
Nathan Homer Knorr in 1942. Under his presidency the
work expanded into at least "lands and islands of the sea."
Knorr died in June 1977. He has been succeeded by Frederick Franz, a Jehovah's Witness since 1913.

<h2>Sources of Authority</h2>

"Let God have the say as to what is the truth that sets
men free" (LG 9). "Accept His Word, the Bible, as the
truth" (LG 9). By these and by similar statements the
Jehovah's Witnesses purport to reveal their devotion to the
Bible. It is "Jehovah's God's written word to mankind, re-
vealing himself and expressing his purpose" (MS 36).

Actually, the ultimate source of authority is the Word of
God as translated and interpreted in voluminous writings of the organization. As stated by Pastor Russell concerning his *Studies in the Scriptures,* "People cannot see
the divine plan by studying the Bible itself."[5] The *Studies*
contain this declaration: "Be it known that no other system of theology even claims, or has ever attempted to har-
monize in itself *every* statement of the Bible, yet nothing
short of this can we claim."[6] The *New World Translation
of the Holy Scriptures* was published by the Watchtower
Bible and Tract Society in 1961. The title page states that
the translation is "rendered from the Original Languages
by the New World Bible Translation Committee." It is a

5. *Watchtower,* September 15, 1910. Quoted by J. Oswald Sanders,
   *Cults and Isms* (Grand Rapids: Zondervan, 1962), p. 79.
6. Charles Taze Russell, *Studies in the Scriptures* (Allegheny, Pa.
   Watchtower Bible and Tract Society, 1907), 1:348.

biased translation, made to verify predetermined doctrines. As Dr. Anthony A. Hoekema writes, "Many of the peculiar teachings of the Watchtower Society are smuggled into the text of the Bible itself."[7] Unwarranted liberties are taken in the English translation to substantiate teaching which is not in keeping with that of historic Christianity but is dogmatically stated in Jehovah's-Witness writings.

For instance, the book *Make Sure of All Things* categorically declares that "the Holy Spirit is NOT a person" (MS 389). Therefore the word *spirit*, indicating the Holy Spirit, is *never* capitalized. Again, since the deity of Jesus Christ is denied, John 1:1 is translated, "In the beginning the Word was . . . and the Word was a god." It has been pointed out that in Colossians 1:15-17 the word "other" has been inserted, without warrant, four times. This is done in order to put Jesus Christ on a level with "other" created things. Philippians 2:6 is another flagrantly false translation. It reads: "[Christ Jesus] although he was existing in God's form, gave no consideration to a seizure, namely, that he should be equal to God." The obvious meaning is that Christ was not equal with God, and did not choose to be.

These examples are given to indicate that the source of authority for Jehovah's Witnesses is not the Bible, but the Bible as interpreted by Russell, Rutherford, and their followers. Russell's "sanctified common sense" rejected the mystery of the Trinity, and with it he eliminated the very person of the Holy Spirit, who convicts of sin (John 16:8), and denigrated the deity of the Son, without which there can be no atonement. (Further information relative to Jehovah's-Witness teaching about the Holy Spirit and the Son is given below, under "THE DOCTRINE OF GOD" and "THE DOCTRINE OF JESUS CHRIST.")

7. Anthony A. Hoekema, *The Four Major Cults* (Grand Rapids: Eerdmans, 1963), pp. 238-39.

## THE DOCTRINE OF GOD

The name *Jehovah* means "the Purposer." He is the only
true God, "and is now working out his purpose of vindicating his name and sovereignty and blessing all faithful
mankind through his kingdom" (MS 193). He is *not* a
triune god, which "false doctrine would deny his almighty
supremacy" (MS 188). The doctrine of the Trinity originated in "ancient Babylonish paganism" (MS 386).

A. Who is Jehovah? This question, asked by Pharaoh of
Egypt, epitomizes the attitude of the world today. It began with the rebellion in Eden, which "called into question Jehovah's position as supreme sovereign."[8] Could Jehovah create a people who would serve Him faithfully in
total obedience? This was the primary issue even before
creation. That the answer is positive is being demonstrated by His "witnesses" as they are declaring His name
throughout the earth.

B. Jehovah is *one* person. His principal attributes are
love, wisdom, justice, and power. At one time all alone in
the universal space, He was self-contained and never lonely.[9] He is above all; He is supreme sovereign of the universe. He is omniscient, but *not* omnipresent, although His
power extends everywhere (MS 191). The doctrine of the
Trinity is brushed aside as being "false, unbiblical." Proof
of this involves, for the most part, denial of the equality of
the Son and the Father. The doctrinal handbook *Make
Sure of All Things* (1953 edition, revised in 1957) succinctly states, "Jesus Inferior to Jehovah," "Jehovah is Christ's
God" (MS 387-88). Added to this is the consistent denial
of the personality of the Holy Spirit.

C. The Holy Spirit is *not* a person; rather, He is subject
to God (MS 387-88). The Spirit is defined as "Jehovah's in-

8. Virgilius Ferm, ed., *Religion in the Twentieth Century* (New York:
   Philosophical Library, 1948), p. 388.
9. *New Heavens and a New Earth* (Brooklyn: Watchtower Bible and
   Tract Society, 1953), p. 21 (hereafter cited as NH).

visible energizing force . . . that produces visible results . . . experienced by men" (MS 360). Thus in the New World Translation of the Holy Scriptures Genesis 1:2 reads, in part, "and God's active force was moving to and fro over the surface of the waters." As indicated above, in the *New World Translation* references to the Holy Spirit are never capitalized. There is no attempt to explain the Spirit's activities as helper, guide, advocate, and comforter, nor is it shown how He convicts of sin, speaks to and through believers, may be grieved, and so forth. (See John 14:16-17, 26; 16:7-15; Acts 13:2; Eph. 4:30; and many other verses.)

## THE DOCTRINE OF CREATION

Jehovah God created all that exists. He, the great First Cause, brought into existence all that is material and spiritual in the universe. In the divine order, there were three stages in creation:

A. The only-begotten Son was the first creation. Jesus Christ is God's first creation. Having received life directly from God "unassisted," he was given "priority and preeminence among all God's creatures."[10] By this creation, Jehovah God became a father. Being endowed with wisdom, the Son became the master workman, the co-worker with Jehovah through whom all else came into existence.

B. Angels, of different ranks, were created next. Shortly after the "dawn of creation," Lucifer, son of the morning, was brought into being. He and the only-begotten Son were the princes, and were called "morning stars," who worked together and "sang together."[11] (See Job 38:7.) Then all other spirit sons of God, seraphim, cherubim, and angels (messengers), were brought forth "perfect, glorious, and holy."[12] They are numbered in the hundreds of mil-

10. *The New World* (Brooklyn: Watchtower Bible and Tract Society, 1942), p. 16.
11. Ibid., p. 18.
12. Ibid., p. 24.

lions, all organized and placed in positions of service.

C. Finally, the heavens and earth were created. At God's command, his "mighty Son, the Word," began to adorn the fathomless depths of space with the material creation."[13] Billions of milky ways and galaxies of stars! It should be noted that any suggestion of evolution is untenable. However, the "silence" of Genesis 1:1 "may allow" for the estimate of "modern science" that the average age of the Milky Way is 3 to 4 billion years (NH 34-35).

Of interest is the calculation that each of the Creator's workdays was 7,000 years long. Reckoning that God's "sabbath rest" began some 6,000 years ago, the Battle of Armageddon is near "and Christ's reign of 1,000 years will begin immediately after it." The Sabbath rest is therefore 7,000 years long. On this basis, man was "put on the earth toward the end of 42,000 years of earth's preparation" (LG 168).

### THE DOCTRINE OF JESUS CHRIST

"Jesus, the Christ, a created individual, is the second greatest Personage of the universe. Jehovah God and Jesus together constitute the Superior Authorities" (MS 207).

The consistent and vehement denial of the deity of Christ is an outstanding feature of this system. In that denial, Jehovah's Witnesses have revived the ancient heresy known as Arianism. To the Witnesses, Jesus Christ was a Jew whose life and teachings have affected the course of all human history. He was one who had a wonderful past before he appeared on earth. But he was not Jehovah God, nor was he equal with Jehovah God. In fact, he was known as Michael, the archangel! (NH 28).

The following headings are taken from pages 207-10 of *Make Sure of All Things* (revised April 1, 1957), which sets

13. *The Truth Shall Make You Free* (Brooklyn: Watchtower Bible and Tract Society, 1943), p. 54.

forth seventy principal themes and gives a "balanced picture" of the belief of Jehovah's Witnesses:

A. *First-born Son of God, a Spirit.* Jesus Christ was a
spirit person, the most beloved and most favored of all
creation. He was the Word, or the Logos. "As such, he
was a god, but not the Almighty God, who is Jehovah"
(LG 33). Note likewise that he did not possess immortality (deathlessness).

B. *Lesser than Jehovah.* That Jesus Christ is lesser than
Jehovah is substantiated by an unjustifiable translation of
Philippians 2:6. "Christ Jesus . . . gave no consideration to
a seizure, namely, that he should be equal to God." That
is, "he did not follow the course of the Devil and plot and
scheme to make himself like or equal to the Most High
God" (LG 34-35). Reference is also made to the errone-
ous, indefensible translation of John 1:1, "In the beginning
was the Word . . . and the Word was a god." While seeking
to deprive the Word of equality with the Father, it actually makes Jehovah's Witnesses to be polytheistic.[14]

C. *Born as a Human Son of God, Oct., 2 B.C.* "At the
time that the young woman conceived by the miracle-
working power of Almighty God then the life of the Son of
God was transferred from his glorious position with God
his Father in heaven to the embryo of a human" (LG 36).
To call this an "incarnation of God" is "unscriptural," for
"the Son of God laid aside completely his spirit existence."[15] He was born as a mere human creature, the "full
equal of the perfect Adam in Eden, sinless and possessed
of the right to perfect human life in Paradise."[16] Jesus forfeited that right in order to become the basis of redemption, as will be noted under "THE DOCTRINE OF SALVATION."

D. *Became the Messiah Seed in Fall, A.D. 29.* By his

14. See Metzger.
15. *The Truth Shall Make You Free*, pp. 245-46.
16. Ibid., p. 249.

water baptism, Jesus indicated his submission to do God's
will. God thereupon consecrated Him by His "holy spirit"
and acknowledged Him as His beloved Son. God "begot
Jesus to be his spiritual Son once more instead of a human
Son" (LG 38). Jesus was anointed to be the long-promised King in God's Kingdom—and to become the Messiah.
Henceforth, he was Jesus Christ, or Jesus the Anointed.

   E. *Died on Stake as Ransomer in Spring, A.D. 33.* By
definition, the cross is a symbol falsely used to represent
Christianity. Jesus was not crucified on a cross; rather, He
was impaled on a stake. This stake is depicted as a single
upright pole, with no crossbar.

   When John the Baptist said, "Behold the Lamb.of God"
(John 1:36), he showed the *secondary* purpose for which
the Son of God came to earth—that is, to die for sinful men.

   F. *Resurrected Immortal on Third Day.* On the third
day, Jesus' immortal Father, Jehovah God, raised Him
from the dead, not as a human Son, but as a mighty immortal *spirit* Son. "For forty days thereafter he materialized,
as angels before him had done, to show himself alive to his
disciples as witnesses" (LG 40). God raised Him to death-
less heavenly life as a glorious spirit creature, exalted to be
next highest to Himself, the Most High God.

   It is to be observed that the materialization of Jesus'
body after the resurrection was a temporary thing. What
became of his physical body? "We know nothing about
what became of it, except that it did not decay or corrupt.
. . . Whether it was dissolved into gases or whether it is
preserved somewhere as a grand memorial of God's love . . .
no one knows."[17]

   Since there is no bodily resurrection, there can be no
second coming in the scriptural sense of that term.

17. Russell, 2:129.

## THE DOCTRINE OF MAN

Toward the end of the sixth creative day, nearly 42,000 years after the beginning of creation, God made man in His own image. Man was given dominion over the earth and its forms of life, with the attributes of wisdom, justice, love, and power. (See above under "THE DOCTRINE OF CREATION.")

A. 1. Man *is* a soul. He consists of a "body together with the life principle or life force activating it" (MS 349). This is a fundamental precept of Jehovah's Witnesses. "Man has no soul within him that is separate and distinct from his human body, and that could exist independently, should the dissolution of the body occur."[18] Death is simply cessation of existence.

2. Man is *not* immortal, any more than are fish, birds, or animals. All are "earthly souls," having organisms of flesh which are "kept living by means of blood circulating in their systems" (MS 349). That is, man does not possess, in any sense, the quality of deathlessness, or incorruptibility. Such a teaching is held to have been originated by Satan in the Garden. Note, above, that even Jesus Christ was not given immortality until the time of the resurrection. Angels also are mortal and destructible.

It should be underlined that orthodox Christianity maintains the doctrine of the inherent immortality of human souls. Genesis 2:7 states that God formed man of the dust of the earth and breathed into his nostrils the breath of life. The body, created from the dust, is mortal and subject to death (separation of soul from body); the soul (the breath of life), is immortal, indestructible, yet subject to spiritual death (separation from God). Man sinned. Lest he eat of the tree of life and thus gain immortality of the body, he was expelled from the Garden of Eden (Gen. 3: 22-23).

18. MS 349; see also *The Truth Shall Make You Free*, p. 75.

3. Immortality as given as a reward for faithfulness to Christ. But it must be noted that *only* the 144,000 can ever receive immortality. Immortality is inseparably linked with the kingdom of heaven, and flesh and blood creatures cannot enter. *Human* souls can only dwell forever on the earth. (See below—the 144,000.)

B. 1. Had Adam not sinned, he would have lived on earth forever in his mortal state. So would all his children.

2. By Adam's disobedience, the sentence of death was passed upon all mankind. Death is called soul-sleep, the "termination of existence, utter cessation of conscious, intellectual or physical activity" of any kind (MS 86). In this connection, note that the resurrection of the body is thus actually re-creation according to the "memory" of God, not restoration of the "original identical body" (MS 311).

Figuring on the basis that one of God's ways of measuring time reckons "one day . . . as a thousand years" (2 Pet. 3:8), it is declared that Adam actually died during the day in which he sinned. He died when he was 930 years old, in the year 309 B.C.E. (Before Our Common Era). He literally ceased to exist, "without hope of resurrection."[19]

3. When Satan induced man to sin, he actually challenged God. Could Jehovah put on earth a man who could not be turned away from Him? God's sovereignty was impugned, and thus the vindication of His name became an issue before the universe.

### The Doctrine of Salvation

"Salvation is the deliverance from the destructive power of sin, a redemption from the ultimate end of sin which is everlasting death, annihilation" (MS 330).

A. The Ransom paid for all. The Fall brought death

19. *Things in Which It Is Impossible for God to Lie* (Brooklyn: Watchtower Bible and Tract Society), pp. 177-78.

to all men, and the possibility of perfect human life with all its rights and earthly prospects was lost. But on the cross Christ made atonement for sin. That is, He provided a ransom which canceled death and gave to man *the opportunity to receive* the gift of life. It must be noted carefully that the ransom price was "his human life poured out in willing sacrifice" (LG 116). He did not deserve to die. But His perfect human life with all its *earthly* prospects and rights was laid down in death, and *"was not taken back* by Jesus at His resurrection, for he was raised a divine spirit creature."[20] He willingly forfeited His perfect human life on earth and thus offset the inherited condemnation for Adam's family. He exchanged "his human existence for the spirit existence, and by relinquishing His right to live, he secured man an opportunity to live" in the paradise that will be located on the earth.[21] He made it possible for most men to attain salvation.

B. The ransom does not avail for all. Salvation is a goal to be attained by those who faithfully carry out their dedication to do God's will. It is a goal made possible by the atonement of Christ, but it is guaranteed only to the faithful ones who endure to the end. Adam is characteristic of those not included among the ransomed. He deliberately forfeited the perfect life God had given him. Eve did likewise. The people of Noah's day, those who lived in Sodom, the religious hypocrites of Jesus' day, and those who are killed at Armageddon are beyond redemption. They have received, or will receive, a "destruction that lasts forever"[22]—eternal annihilation.

C. Only the 144,000 will share in heavenly glory with Jesus Christ. (All other Jehovah's Witnesses will enjoy the blessings of life on the earth.)

20. John H. Gerstner, *The Theology of the Major Sects* (Grand Rapids: Baker, 1960), p. 165.
21. Ibid.
22. *From Paradise Lost to Paradise Regained*, p. 202.

We are told that God had predestinated the "requirements and the qualifications" of this heavenly class before
the foundation of the world. The number was also foreordained, but not revealed until John wrote Revelation
7:4 and 14:1-3. This amazing misinterpretation of Scripture gives exclusively to these "chosen ones" all the names
and rights given in the Bible to the saints. The 144,000
constitute the bride, the Lamb's wife. They are the elect,
the holy nation, the royal priesthood. They only are
anointed with God's spirit, and are members of the body,
the church. Designated requirements are:

1. They must exercise faith in God's provision, the shed
blood of Christ. This, of course, includes baptism, sym-
bolizing dedication. "Christ Jesus then acts as an advocate,
covering the sins of such dedicated one by the merit of his
sacrifice. The dedicated one is *now* in position to be justi-
fied or declared righteous by God, and thus he has access
to God through Christ Jesus. He has an acceptable body
and the right to perfect life on earth, and all this can be
presented for sacrifice with Christ Jesus" (LG 298-99,
italics added).

2. "God now . . . causes his active force or holy spirit to
act upon them so as to bring them forth as spiritual sons
with the hope of life in the heavens, and he acknowledges
them as his sons" (LG 300). (See above—the baptism of
Jesus.)

3. They must "demonstrate their dependability by carry-
ing out their dedication faithfully until death" (LG 301).
"If they resist Satan and his world and maintain integrity
until death, they are assured of the 'crown of life,' immortality, divine nature" (LG 302).

The apostles were the first members of this group.

D. The other sheep are promised everlasting life on
earth. These are the unnumbered persons now working as
Jehovah's Witnesses. For them there is no suggestion of

justification or regeneration. They must have faith in Jesus Christ, preceded by repentance from sin. Then they must be baptized by immersion. This baptism symbolizes complete dedication and is a declaration of their stand for God's universal sovereignty. This "baptism into the greater Noah" saves them now, and later it will keep them saved through Armageddon, "*provided* . . . they abide in him, keeping their good conscience through faith and loyal service" (NH 311).

The Jehovah's Witness is never given a clear title to salvation. Every suggestion of assurance is qualified by the absolute requirement of continuance in faith, endurance, obedience, and witnessing.

> According to Watchtower teaching, one of four possible destinies awaits a person when he dies: (1) he may remain in the condition of non-existence into which death has plunged him (as in the case of Adam, Cain, Judas, and others beyond redemption); (2) he may be "raised" with a "spirit body," thus receiving immortality, after which he will go directly to heaven to reign there with Christ (as one of the 144,000); (3) he may be raised with a physical body and then, after having passed the millennial tests, receive everlasting life on the renewed earth; or (4) he may, after having been raised with a physical body, still fail to pass the millennial tests, and thus eventually be annihilated.[23]

## The Doctrine of Things to Come

It should be noted that the Kingdom of God is *entirely heavenly*. It is a Sovereign-empowered theocratic government with Jehovah himself as the great Everlasting King. Christ Jesus is co-regent, with the 144,000 as associate kings. "The term also is used to refer to the realm over which the Kingdom government exercises control" (MS 226).

23. Hoekema, p. 295.

A. In 1914 the Kingdom began operation in full with the enthronement of Christ in the heavens.

In that year Christ received his "never-to-be-destroyed" Kingdom. This marked the end of the "appointed times of the nations"[24] and the time of the end of this world began. This is proved by the following amazing compilation of Bible passages:

(1) Daniel 4:16—The "appointed times of the nations" is 7 times.

(2) Revelation 12:6, 14—A time, times, and half a time means 3½ times, or half of 7 times. 3½ times equal 1,260 days (v. 6); therefore 7 times would be 2,520 days.

(3) Numbers 14:34; Ezekiel 4:6 set God's rule as "a day for a year." Therefore, 2,520 days mean 2,520 years!

In 607 B.C. Jerusalem was captured by Babylon, to begin the "times of the nations." Proceeding 2,520 years from 607 B.C. brings us to A.D. 1914, the year in which Christ's "second coming" took place. At that time, "the devil and his angels were hurled down to earth, and all kinds of trouble ensued for the people on the earth."[25] World War I is proof of this!

B. In 1918 two major events took place:

1. Jesus entered the "spiritual temple, and began to cleanse it." This marked the period of judgment and inspection of his spirit-begotten followers—that is, the 144,000 who had died. These were now "raised with spirit-bodies to join him at the spiritual temple" (LG 203). This is the *first resurrection*. Included within this resurrection are all members of the 144,000 who die subsequent to 1918. They are given spiritual bodies immediately at death—provided, of course, that they have maintained integrity!

2. The judgment of the nations began. The people liv-

24. *From Paradise Lost to Paradise Regained,* p. 173.
25. Ibid., p. 176.

ing in the world are being divided into "the sheep and goats" (Matt. 25:31-46). The resurrected members of the 144,000 are associated with Christ as judges. The basis of judgment is the individual attitude toward Jehovah's Witnesses and their message.

C. The Battle of Armageddon is the next great event in history. It is imminent! This is "the battle of Jehovah God Almighty in which his executive officer Christ Jesus leads invisible forces of righteousness to destroy Satan and his demonic and human organization, eliminating wickedness from the universe and vindicating Jehovah's universal sovereignty" (MS 24). "Organized religion," the great harlot of Revelation 17:1-3, will lead all nations as part of Satan's organization in heaven and earth. The beast of Revelation 17:3 is the United Nations! It was (as the League of Nations), is not (during World War II), and has ascended (as the U.N.) (see Rev. 17:8).

Armageddon does not mean a literal place. Megiddo is symbolic. "Armageddon refers to God's war by which he destroys the world at the accomplished end."[26] It is said that over "two billion people will die."[27] Satan will be crushed and cast into the abyss for 1,000 years (Rev. 20:1-3). This abyss is a "deathlike state of inactivity," like the state Jesus Himself was in when He died. Thus Genesis 3:15 is fulfilled!

D. Armageddon survivors will enter the Millennium on earth. The new earth (new human society under new social arrangements) will be governed by the New Heavens (Christ Jesus and the 144,000). "There will be no evil, no disease, nor aches nor pains . . . but lasting peace and unity—one worship of Jehovah" (LG 26). Vigorous, energetic youth will be the lot of every faithful human. And Armageddon survivors will marry and have children.

26. *From Paradise Lost to Paradise Regained*, p. 204.
27. *You May Survive Armageddon into God's New World* (Brooklyn: Watchtower Bible and Tract Society, 1955),

When, according to the divine mandate, the earth is full to
capacity, "people will stop having children."[28] Every child
will have full opportunity for life through Christ the King
but "any not desiring to serve Jehovah will be executed"
(LG 269).

E. There will be two resurrections early in the Millennium. The first persons to be raised to life on earth with
physical bodies will be Jehovah's faithful witnesses of
pre-Christian times. These are the Old Testament faithful,
such as Enoch, Noah, Abraham, David, and so forth. They
will become direct children of Christ the King and will be
princes on the earth. Included with them will be "other
sheep" who may have died before Armageddon.

Next will be the resurrection of those who "wanted to do
right, but died without opportunity to hear, or learn. . . .
Decent . . . sincere people."[29] They will be taught the
truth and judged according to what they do about it. If
they obey God's commands, they will get life; if not, they
will go to everlasting death, as Adam did. *Let God be True*
optimistically states that "the greater mass of humankind
will find life here on earth amid paradise conditions" (LG
279).

Noteworthy is the teaching that the Millennium is a
"1,000-Year Day of Test," or judgment. "All earth's inhabitants in the new world of righteousness" will be judged
But they will not be judged on the basis of their past deeds,
"but on the basis of what their deeds will be during the
judgment day" (LG 293).

F. The final test, or judgment, will come when Satan,
the devil, is loosed (Rev. 20:7-9). By deceit, he will gain
a large following and lead a final rebellion against Jehovah.
Christ the King steps aside "for the Supreme Judge, Jehovah God, to make the test" (NH 353). All the rebels, with

28. *From Paradise Lost to Paradise Regained*, p. 225.
29. Ibid. p. 229.

Satan and his demons, will be cast into the lake of fire and sulphur, Gehenna. That is, "they are disintegrated, annihilated, as if they had never existed before" (NH 355).

The issue of Jehovah's universal sovereignty will have been settled for good, forever.

G. The 144,000 having been raised in spirit-bodies, will remain in heaven for eternity. They are "joint-heirs and co-rulers" with Christ, in Jehovah's theocracy. The "other sheep" will remain on earth, entering "upon an eternity of paradisaic happiness in the ever-abiding new earth" (NH 360). "Absolute and endless destruction" is the doom of all others.

# 3

## Sun Myung Moon's Unification Church

"WE NOW HAVE THE MEANS TO HEAL all modern-day human problems, exalt every human soul, and bring the kingdom of God within the reach of every man."[1] This all-embracing claim is based upon "new revelations from God" which were given to the Reverend Sun Myung Moon, founder of the Unification Church (The Holy Spirit Association for the Unification of World Christianity, Inc.). Briefly told, this new interpretation of the Bible teaches that God created the world of goodness to last forever. But Satan seduced Eve and brought about the Fall of man, and God's good world ended abruptly. Ever since, God has been trying to rectify His creation, but has not yet succeeded. He has worked through chosen men, His champions. All were men of self-denial, but all failed to find acceptance with men. Abel, Noah, Abraham, Jacob, Moses, yes, and Jesus Christ, they all failed. "The death of Jesus was neither his will nor his fault. . . . [It was] murder, and his body was taken by Satan" (CC 104). Having failed as He did, Jesus will come again as the Lord of the second advent. At first He will suffer and be rejected. But He will find His chosen bride; they will become the True Parents; and heaven on earth will be literally achieved.

1. Sun Myung Moon, *Christianity in Crisis* (Washington, D.C.: Holy Spirit Association for the Unification of World Christianity, 1974), p. IX (hereafter cited as CC).

## The Founder

Sun Myung Moon was born in Korea on January 6, 1920. With his family members, he was "converted" to Christianity at the age of ten. On Easter morning, 1936, while deep in prayer, he had a vision. Jesus appeared to him and told him that he had been chosen to complete the mission which He had started two thousand years ago. God, it appeared, was lonely, and longed for fellowship with man.

By 1944 he had gained a following in North Korea. He was, however, badly treated by the Communist regime, and apparently he was rescued from execution by the U.N. forces in 1950. Later that year he began to teach his Divine Principle. In 1954 he officially established his new church, calling it The Holy Spirit Association for the Unification of World Christianity, or simply The Unification Church. There are shadows over certain reputed sex practices in the early days of the church, as there are over Moon's own marital affairs. However, in 1960 he was married to his present wife, who is either his fourth or second, depending on which report one believes. They have nine children.

"The union between Sun Myung Moon and Hak Ja Han is called 'The Marriage of the Lamb.' Moon is called 'the Father of the universe' and his wife is called the 'Mother of the universe.' Consequently their [nine] children are considered to be sinless. Together, the parents and children are heralding the coming perfection of humanity."[2]

## Sources of Authority

A. The Holy Bible is one of the Unification Church's sources of authority—but the Bible is subject to new interpretation based upon the revelations given to Mr. Moon.

---

2. J. Isamu Yamamoto, *The Puppet Master* (Downers Grove, Ill.: InterVarsity, 1977), p. 21.

B. *The Divine Principle*[3] is "a set of principles based on the patterns which Rev. Moon found in the Bible during his years of search" (CC 120). It is a weighty volume of 536 pages, translated into English from Korean. In it are the basic doctrines of the Unification Church. Being considered only part of the new truth, it will be enhanced as expected "deeper parts of the truth will be continually revealed." The general introduction to this book declares that

> with the fullness of time, God has sent His messenger to resolve the fundamental questions of life and the universe. His name is Sun Myung Moon. For many decades, he wandered in a vast spiritual world in search of the ultimate truth. On this path, he endured suffering unimagined by anyone in human history. . . . He fought alone against myriads of Satanic forces, both in the spiritual and physical worlds, and finally triumphed over them all. In this way, he came in contact with many saints in Paradise and with Jesus, and thus brought into light all the heavenly secrets through his communion with God [DP 16].

### THE DOCTRINE OF GOD AND MAN

"God Himself told me that the most basic and central truth of this universe is that *God is the Father and we are His children*" (CC 9). God is, by definition, the creator of all things. He is the absolute reality, eternally self-existent, transcendent of time and space. However, "being the first Cause of all creation, [God] also exists because of a reciprocal relationship between the dual characteristics of positivity and negativity" (DP 24). Thus, before creating the universe, God was incomplete. He existed only as the internal masculine subject, and He created the universe as His external feminine object. This theory is obviously re-

3. Sun Myung Moon, *The Divine Principle* (Washington, D.C.: Holy Spirit Association for the Unification of World Christianity, 1973) (hereafter cited as DP).

lated to the book *I Ching,* of the Taoist religion. In it the
basic fundamental of the universe is the constant inter-
play between the Yang and Yin (positivity and negativity).

From this comes the principle that God cannot exist
without man, as man cannot exist without God. There cannot be love without a lover and a beloved. Even God needs
"to share, to have give and take with someone in a reciprocal relationship. . . . That is why God created His object,
man" (CC 4). Further, "God and man are one. Man is incarnate God." As such, man "is as important in value as
God Himself" (CC 5).

Thus it is that man was created in the image of God in
order to fulfill this need in God. And this relationship is
fulfilled when man lives in full accord with the will of God,
in union with God. But as God finds his joy in giving Himself in and for His creation, so He gave the pattern for the
universe and for man. We are to live our lives for others.
Thus the circle is complete. And "without this give and
take action between subject and object . . . nothing endures
for eternity" (CC 16). Further, heaven (the Kingdom of
God) will be on earth when there is God-involvement in
every human relationship. (See "SALVATION AND THE KING-
DOM OF GOD ON EARTH.")

### THE DOCTRINE OF THE FALL OF MAN

God had poured His soul into the creation of His master-
piece, man. He gave "100% of Himself." The circle was
to be complete, each giving of himself for the other. But
selfishness emerged and the circle was broken. In fact, it
was never completed. Eve became Satan's first victim;
then Adam was ensnared; and God was isolated in the Garden of Eden. How did it happen?

A. Lucifer was an archangel, able to "monopolize God's
love as mediator between God and the angelic world" (DP
78). When God loved Adam and Eve, Lucifer resented it.

He seduced Eve, and by the act of sexual intercourse she "received certain elements from Lucifer." Eve, hoping to get rid of those elements, seduced Adam. However, she merely passed them on to him, and thus they were transmitted to all their descendants. The elements were fear, which came from a guilty conscience, and wisdom that was immature.

B. The Fall was both *spiritual*, through the blood relationship between the angel and Eve, and *physical*, through the blood relationship between Eve and Adam. In the spiritual fall, Eve submitted to Satan, and "received the elements of fear (from a guilty conscience), and wisdom enabling her to perceive that her intended spouse . . . was Adam" (DP 79). The physical Fall was caused because the relationship between Adam and Eve centered on Satan. Thus the "elements" were inherited by Adam and passed on to their descendants. Instead of the good lineage of God, the evil lineage of Satan was multiplied. This, actually, is what God has been seeking to rectify ever since. And He will, it appears, through the True Parents who will have sinless children!

God's work has been that of restoration. In seeking to destroy the world of evil and re-create the world of goodness, He needs tools. "The religions of the world have served as these tools for God." Christianity is the "most progressive religion because it teaches sacrificial love and duty in supreme form" (CC 18). The Lord of the Second Advent, who will come as the central figure of Christianity, will accomplish the ultimate purpose of all the religions.

### THE DOCTRINE OF THE SAVIOR, JESUS CHRIST

The basic questions are: Who was Jesus Christ? What did He hope to accomplish on earth? Did He succeed? Will He come to earth again? Is Rev. Moon the Lord of the Second Advent?

A. Who was Jesus Christ? In *The Divine Principle,* the answer is not clear. It is stated that He was the incarnation of the Word, and that he may well be called the Creator. This means, however, that he was a man who had fulfilled the purpose of creation, and "does not signify that he was the Creator Himself" (DP 211). "As a man [Jesus was] no different from us except for the fact that he was without original sin" (DP 212).

At present He is in the spirit world as a divine-spirit-man with his disciples, but He has attained a higher level of being than they. "The fact that he called on God for help, was tempted by Satan, and finally crucified by the evil force" (DP 212) makes it clear that Jesus was not God himself. "He was the one who lived God's ideal in fullest realization" (CC 12). With this in mind, it is to be noted that "a perfected man, in light of the purpose of creation, should become perfect (Mt. 5:48); thus, he is so valuable as to even possess deity! Since God is eternal, man, who was created as His substantial object, should also become eternal, after his perfection" (DP 209). "Jesus was a man who had attained the purpose of creation" (DP 290). "In light of his attained deity, he may well be called God. Nevertheless he can by no means be called God himself" (DP 210-11).

B. Why did He come to earth? He came, as a man, to be the True Parent of mankind. He came as Messiah, to save fallen man. This means that He came to restore men as citizens of the Heavenly Kingdom. It is to be remembered that God created man for fellowship. Man was to be the means of fulfilling God in the subject-object relationship. The first Adam had failed. Jesus was the Second Adam. He was to have found His chosen bride, the Second Eve, and "to bring forth upon this earth his own sinless children. Thus the Second Adam and Second Eve would become the

True Parents for mankind, and all mankind would have found life by grafting on to them" (CC 28).

C. Did He succeed? No. In spite of the fact that the "field had been prepared" in Israel, He did not find acceptance as Messiah. He did not come to die on the cross. That was not in the predestinative will of God. In fact, Christ "prayed desperately" that it might not take place. He died "a reluctant death" due to the unbelief of the Jewish people. "His body was invaded by Satan, and he was killed" (DP 148). He failed as other champions had failed.

Mention should be made here of the dismal part played by John the Baptist in this failure. He, the expressed forerunner, was to "accomplish the mission which Elijah had left unaccomplished on earth" (DP 162). He knew that Jesus was the Messiah. But he began to doubt, and then to disbelieve. His rejection of Jesus as Messiah influenced the Jewish people to deny Jesus also.

However, the cross was not all in vain. Without it Christian history could not have existed. "We can never deny the magnitude of the grace of redemption by the cross. . . . [But] the cross has been unable to remove our original sin and restore us as men of the original nature who cannot sin" (DP 142). Nevertheless, through faith in Jesus Christ one experiences "spiritual rebirth." That is, he is saved "spiritually." The explanation is found in this quotation from *The Divine Principle:*

> As it is written (I Cor. 12:3) when we come to believe in Jesus as the Savior through the inspiration of the Holy Spirit, we receive the love of the spiritual True Parents, coming from the give and take action between Jesus, the spiritual True Father, and the Holy Spirit, the spiritual True Mother. Then, through this love, new life is infused into those who believe in Christ, and each is reborn into a new spiritual self. This is called "spiritual rebirth" [DP 216].

D. Will He come to earth the second time? Yes, He will come again as the Third Adam, the Lord of the Second Advent. He will come "in the flesh," as He did the first time. That is, He will not come in clouds of glory. At first, He will suffer many things and be rejected. Some "saints" will recognize Him, and "the Kingdom of Heaven will be first realized in their hearts." With their increase, "the Kingdom of God will gradually appear" (DP 506). This means that He will become the True Parent, and that He will thus bring about the Kingdom of God on earth.

On the basis of Revelation 7:2-4 and 14:1, it has been revealed to Mr. Moon that "Christ will be born in a country in the East—that is, from the rising of the sun—and will place a seal on the foreheads of the 144,000" (DP 520). That nation is Korea. The Korean people will become the Third Israel, "God's elect." (See DP 520-32.)

E. Is Sun Myung Moon the Lord of the Second Advent? From many angles, it would appear that he fits the picture. His birth, his revelations, his wife and family, his Unified Family (the Unification Church), his being hailed as "the Perfect Father" suggest a positive answer to the question. He is openly known as the Master, or Father. "He and his wife are the Perfect Parents who will bring salvation to the world."[4] In his book *The Puppet Master,* J. Isamu Yamamoto quotes from the *120-Day Training Manual* of the Unification Church as follows:

> By loving the Messiah [Moon] and obeying and believing the Messiah more than my own life, and by doing what he requires with great faith, now we can realize the Kingdom of God on earth and in heaven. . . . Father [Moon] is sinless, Mother [Moon's wife] is sinless, and their children are sinless. This is called the Messiah's family; this was established in 1967, on December 31. . . . Through Father [Moon] and Mother [his wife] we can be born

4. Yamamoto, p. 65.

anew, sinlessly. . . . Father is given authority here on earth by God to forgive sins.[5]

Apparently the claim to Messiahship is not made publicly. But the "inner teachings" support the belief that Moon is Messiah, the Lord of the Second Advent. Mr. Yamamoto quotes further from the *120-Day Training Manual:* "Father is visible God."[6]

It might be added that such fulfillment of the second coming of Christ in Mr. Moon follows a pattern. There is the accepted principle that "spirit-men . . . must come to earth again and fulfil the responsibility they left unaccomplished in their physical life on earth through the physical bodies of earthly men" (DP 181). Elijah's return in John the Baptist is cited as proof of this.

### THE DOCTRINE OF SALVATION, AND THE DOCTRINE OF THE KINGDOM OF GOD ON EARTH

A. Salvation, as *The Divine Principle* handles it, is a complex subject. The events in the Garden of Eden caused man to fall in two ways: spiritually and physically. Christ's work of redemption on the cross accomplished "spiritual salvation" for man. But it did not accomplish his physical salvation. Original sin remained in all men. This must be annihilated in order for the Kingdom of God to be established on earth. In *The Divine Principle* it is stated that "if Jesus had not been crucified, he would have accomplished the providence of salvation both spiritually and physically. He would have established the Kingdom of Heaven on earth which would last forever" (DP 147). The salvation of spirit and body is called also the "providence of restoration." But Christ failed, and "even the saints redeemed by the cross have had to continue to fight against original sin" (DP 149).

5. Ibid., p. 54.
6. Ibid., p. 87.

Christ's coming as Lord of the Second Advent is to be with the purpose of completing His unfinished work. He must come as the True Parent. And when the "True Father and True Mother become one, and love each other, God would come down and become one with them on earth."[7] Because God is spiritual only, he creates a central person, or persons, through whom mankind can receive rebirth. The True Parents give spiritual life. And this is presently realized "by loving the Messiah [Moon] and obeying and believing the Messiah more than my own life, and by doing what he requires with great faith."[8]

The "doing what he requires" is related to restoration through indemnity. This is a complex matter "revealed" at length in *The Divine Principle*. "The providence of restoration cannot be fulfilled by God's power alone, but it is to be fulfilled by man's joint action with God" (DP 283). This spells *works* and explains somewhat the hours spent by the "Moonies" as they sell flowers in public places. Testimonials tell of days that start at 5:00 A.M. and rarely end before midnight. In addition, "we must first establish direct rapport with God in spirit through ardent prayer, and next, we must understand the truth through correct reading of the Bible" (DP 152). This latter point may account for the seemingly interminable public and private lectures to which the young followers are subjected.

B. It is taught that bodies are only temporal dwellings for spirits. The human body, once it is corrupted and decomposed, cannot be resurrected into its original state. Further, "it is not necessary for a spirit man to resume his flesh, when there is a vast spirit world where he is supposed to go and live forever" (DP 170).

Therefore, resurrection means the phenomena occurring

7. Frederick Sontag, *Sun Myung Moon* (Nashville: Abingdon, 1977), p. 119.
8. Yamamoto, p. 54. Quoted from the *120-Day Training Manual*, p. 328.

in the process of man's restoration, according to the providence of restoration, from the state of having fallen under
Satanic dominion, back to the direct dominion of God.
Accordingly, when we repent of our sins, making ourselves better and better, day by day, we are coming closer
to resurrection [DP 170].

In brief, there is no physical resurrection. The resurrected Jesus was not the Jesus who had lived with His disciples. He was a being transcendent of time and space.
He had given up His physical body as a sacrifice.

By devious means, it is explained that "spirit men who
passed away to the spirit world without having perfected
themselves . . . must come again to earth and fulfil the responsibility they left unaccomplished in their physical life
on earth through the physical bodies of earthly men, by
cooperating with earthly saints and helping them fulfil the
same mission" (DP 181). John the Baptist and Elijah "co-
operated" to fulfill the mission Elijah left unaccomplished!

C. There is an elaborate hierarchy of attainment by
which men will achieve entrance into the Kingdom of
Heaven on earth. Fallen man must be raised to a proper
relationship with God by the providence of restoration.
This "perfection" is to be accomplished through three or-
derly stages of growth; the form-spirit stage, the life-spirit
stage, and the divine-spirit stage. Until the time of Jesus,
men attained the form-spirit stage after death by having
kept the Law. Since the cross, men attain the life-spirit
stage (and go to paradise) through faith in the gospel (DP
175). During the time of the Lord of the Second Advent,
"spirit men of this age can attain the divine-spirit stage of
perfect restoration by believing and serving the Lord of
the Second Advent" (DP 175).

Regardless of one's position (stage) in the spirit world,
he can raise his spirit level by intercommunicating with
men on earth. There must be active give and take between

spirit and body in order to produce intermediate and ultimate fulfillment—that is, in order that the divine-spirit
stage might be attained and the Kingdom of Heaven
reached. "The ultimate purpose of God's providence of
restoration is to save all mankind" (DP 190). Hell is a
temporary condition, and is in the world. Paradise is likewise a temporary dwelling place inhabited by men of the
life-spirit stage as they await the opening of the Kingdom
of Heaven. That kingdom is as yet vacant.

D. In Moon's writings, much is said about the Kingdom
of Heaven, or Kingdom of God, on earth. It should have
been established by Jesus when He came the first time.
As we have noted, He failed, but He will succeed when He
comes again. Then, men will live in union and communion
with God, the True Parent. God will be living for men, and
men for God. There will be God-involvement in every relationship. The so-called Four Position Foundation—God,
husband, wife, offspring in perfect give-and-take relationship—will be the base through which God's power will be
channeled into all creation.

Marriage is believed to be essential to this salvation.
Only the male and female together can represent God
totally. The marriage relationship is therefore advocated in
the Unification Church. "In February, 1975, Moon married 1800 couples in Seoul, Korea, from twenty-five countries."[9] "The matching was done by the Master [Moon]
and many of the couples hardly knew or had ever seen each
other before.[10]

Another facet is added to this by the revelation to Moon
that the Holy Spirit is a female. "She came as the True
Mother, that is, the Second Eve" (DP 215). "She also
cleanses the sins of the people in order to restore them, thus
indemnifying the sin committed by Eve" (DP 215).

9. Yamamoto, p. 55.
10. Sontag, p. 167.

As noted above, attainment of a place in the kingdom would appear to be guaranteed to all mankind. It will be a world (on earth) in which God's commands will be conveyed to all His children through the True Parents, and all will work toward one purpose.

The True Parents play a significant role in this. It is frequently indicated that Jesus will come as the Third Adam (Lord of the Second Advent). He will take a bride. The marriage supper of the Lamb will take place. All mankind will find life by being "grafted" into his family.

Mr. and Mrs. Moon are now being called the True Parents. They and their nine children are sinless, and are the beginning of the Kingdom of Heaven on earth.

The earth will be populated by divine-spirit beings living in perfect harmony with God. Thus in the give and take between subject and object, the perfect relationship will be maintained. God will be completely fulfilled in His creation.

❁        ❁        ❁

As a postscript, it is interesting to note that the American president of the Unification Church, Neil Albert Salonen, is quoted as saying that the theology of the church is "still evolving. That's not to say we don't know what we believe, but Rev. Moon is still receiving revelations."[11] He further added that in 1977 the church had an estimated income of $24.7 million. The church owns $20 million worth of property in New York state, half of which is mortgaged. "Members who sell candy and flowers gross an average of $80 per day from sales, and this is the main source of income for the church."[12]

---

11. In *The Christian Reader,* September-October 1978, p. 34.
12. Ibid.

# 4

## Herbert W. Armstrong's Worldwide Church of God

THE WORLDWIDE CHURCH OF GOD owes its beginning and continuance to its founder, Herbert W. Armstrong, and to his son, Garner Ted Armstrong. Born in 1892, Herbert W. Armstrong's particular interest in the Bible began in 1924. A neighbor lady had persuaded Mrs. Armstrong to keep the Sabbath. Herbert W. was motivated to frantic study to prove her wrong. This experience led him out as a preacher with a variety of church groups. Ultimately, in January 1934, the Radio Church of God came into being. This became the Worldwide Church of God. Amazing growth has been fostered by intense salesmanship via publications, radio, and television. Some five hundred local congregations are claimed, with membership represented as 75,000. "The World Tomorrow," the church's television program, claims an audience of 30 million. Radio programs over more than three hundred stations reach additional millions of people. Financially, the "fabulous take" is reported as some $75 million a year. Circulation of the church's monthly magazine, *The Plain Truth* (sent without charge to all who ask for it), is around 2 million. It is published in five languages in 187 countries. The Ambassador College Correspondence Course is available on the same free basis.

Garner Ted Armstrong has been the "silver-tongued spokesman," during recent years, on radio and television.

In 1972 Herbert W. "yanked" Garner Ted off the air and
sent him into exile. No reasons were given. Insiders later
reported that the son was guilty of adultery. Garner Ted
had been head of the church and of the church-owned Ambassador College. Some time later, he was reinstated, but
he was again excommunicated by his father in June 1978.
This was apparently final.

The ousted son has formed a new church, The Church
of God International, apparently hoping to draw dissidents
from his father's domain. News media suggest a power
struggle as being a major factor in the rift, with a financial
crisis aiding further separation. There has been as yet no
indication of any significant defection toward the new
church.

The Worldwide Church of God (Armstrongism) has no
equal as an example of extreme eclecticism coupled with a
blatant claim to originality. "The prophecies and mys-
teries of God, sealed until now, are today revealed to those
whom God has chosen to carry His last message to the
world as a witness."[1] There is only one true church of God.
"All others are counterfeit."[2] And yet it is clearly observ-
able that basic doctrines of the Worldwide Church of God
are similar to those of the Jehovah's Witnesses, Mormonism, et al., and certainly British-Israelism is not unique to
Armstrong.

The basic theory of British-Israelism is that the Anglo-
Saxon countries, Britain and its former empire (including
the United States), are the ten lost tribes of Israel. In
brief, note these points:

1.  God's promise to Abraham was that he should be the
    father of many nations, of whom the Jews were only
    one.

1. Herbert W. Armstrong, *The Book of Revelation Revealed at Last*
   (Pasadena, Calif.: Ambassador College Press, 1959), p. 4.
2. Herman L. Hoeh, *A True History of the True Church* (Pasadena,
   Calif.: Ambassador College Press, 1959), p. 28.

2. God made an "unconditional and unbreakable" covenant with David. The throne of David was to be established forever (2 Sam. 7:13). This throne exists today.
3. Israel lost its identity in 721 B.C., when its people were carried away captive to Assyria, and became known as "the ten lost tribes."
4. Ephraim, which according to Jacob's prophecy was to become a multitude of nations (a commonwealth), is Great Britain.
5. Manasseh is the United States.[3]

Added is the fantasy that the Scottish Stone of Scone (which is placed under the throne in Westminster Abbey) is actually the stone used by Jacob as a pillow at Bethel. It was taken by the prophet Jeremiah to Britain when he took the daughter of Zedekiah to Ireland. Thus Elizabeth II is Queen of Israel! The Saxons (Isaac-son), or British (*Brit* being Hebrew for "covenant" and *ish* meaning *"man"*), are the covenant people!

In the Worldwide Church of God the only recognized source of authority is the Bible. The only true interpretation is that of the Worldwide Church of God.

### THE DOCTRINE OF GOD

God is the creator, the beginner, the one who caused us to have life, and so is called our Father.[4] However, declaring the doctrine of the Trinity to be pagan and false, the Worldwide Church of God emphasizes that "God is a Family, a Kingdom, NOT a limited trinity."[5] Further, "at the present time there are only two beings in the God Family.

3. Herbert W. Armstrong, *The United States and the British Commonwealth in Prophecy* (Pasadena, Calif.: Ambassador College Press, 1954).
4. David Jon Hill, "Why Is God the Father Called a Father?" *Tomorrow's World*, September-October 1970, p. 24.
5. *The Plain Truth*, August 1958, p. 17.

1) God the Father, Father of Jesus Christ, 2) God of Abraham, Isaac, and Jacob, the One who became Jesus Christ, God the Son."[6] However, on the basis that God is reproducing Himself, men are actually begotten (not born) as sons at conversion. As they grow spiritually, they will be "born of God" at the time of the resurrection. For "man was created to literally become God."[7] And "we shall one day be . . . divine as He is divine."[8] To emphasize this further, it is written that we shall actually "generate eternal life intrinsically within ourselves" and "will counsel and advise our Creator-Father."[9] It should be noted that this partakes of Mormon doctrine, but seems to go to a greater extreme.

## THE DOCTRINE OF CHRIST

"Christ has existed from all eternity with the Father. He is one with the Father, but He is subordinate to the Father."[10] The Yahweh (Jehovah) of the Old Testament is Jesus Christ.

Jesus Christ, Yahweh, became man, being born of the virgin Mary. Until that time, He was not the Son. Armstrong's Ambassador College Bible Correspondence Course says:

> Before Christ (the Logos) was conceived in Mary, He was not the "Son of God." He was one of the two original members of the God Kingdom. He, like the one who became the "Father," had existed eternally. But He is nowhere in God's Word referred to as a Son of God prior to His conception in Mary. His human birth was His first birth.[11]

6. "The God Family," *Tomorrow's World*, May 1971.
7. Robert L. Kuhn, "What It Means to Be Equal with GOD," *Tomorrow's World*, April 1971, p. 43.
8. Herbert W. Armstrong, *What Do You Mean—Born Again?* (Pasadena, Calif.: Ambassador College Press, 1962), p. 15.
9. Kuhn, pp. 44-45.
10. Paul N. Benware, *Ambassadors of Armstrongism* (Nutley, N.J.: Presby. & Ref., 1975), p. 44.
11. Ambassador College Bible Correspondence Course, lesson 8.

As a man, He could have sinned, but did not. He "became perfect through the trials and tests of human experience.... He kept God's commandments perfectly, . . . [and] developed the perfection of spiritual character which enabled Him to become our Savior and elder brother."[12] He died as a voluntary sacrifice on the cross to pay the penalty of sin. However, as will be noted later (see "THE DOCTRINE OF SALVATION"), "the blood of Christ does not finally save any man."[13]

Crucified on Wednesday (as is adamantly maintained by Armstrong), Christ was raised again on Saturday, at the end of the Jewish Sabbath. But note that "the resurrected body was no longer human—it was the Christ resurrected, immortal, once again changed! . . . He was . . . converted into immortality, and He is alive forevermore."[14] Having been given immortality, He was now a spiritual Son of God, a divine Being. As to the body, it disappeared.[15] Presumably, in dying, Christ ceased to exist. He was then re-created by God after three days of total extinction.

(Concerning the doctrine of the Holy Spirit, it should be noted that His personality is denied. "The Holy Spirit is the very power of God. *It* expresses the unified, creative will of the God family."[16] In similarity to Jehovah's-Witness teaching, "the Holy Spirit is not a third person of the Godhead as taught by the pagan 'trinity' idea."[17] Note also that God is *not* omnipresent. "The Father and the Son are in definitè locations . . . the spirit proceeds from them

---

12. Ibid., lesson 9.
13. Herbert W. Armstrong, *All About Water Baptism* (Pasadena Calif.: Ambassador College Press, 1972), p. 2.
14. Herbert W. Armstrong, "Why Christ Died—and Rose Again," *The Plain Truth*, April 1963, p. 10.
15. C. Paul Meredith, *If You Die—Will You Live Again?* 1958, 1971, p. 6. Quoted by R. L. Sumner, *Armstrongism* (Brownsburg, Ind.: Biblical Evangelism Press, 1974), p. 113.
16. Ambassador College Bible Correspondence Course, lesson 9.
17. Ibid.

and fills the entire universe."[18] "Whenever we become members of God's begotten family, we receive a portion, a seed or germ, of the Father's Holy Spirit."[19])

## The Doctrine of Man

The account of creation is accepted literally. The creation of man "in the image of God" took place approximately six thousand years ago. The Fall of man was planned and permitted by God. Any other explanation would suggest that Satan outwitted God.

"In its view of man the Worldwide Church of God adopts the view of conditionalism, along with the Seventh-Day Adventists and Jehovah's Witnesses. Conditionalism teaches that man was created as a living soul with the potential for immortality."[20] Holding thus to the teaching of "conditional immortality," the Worldwide Church of God teaches that the condition of all men after death is that of unconsciousness, or "soul sleep." They remain thus until the resurrection of the righteous to immortality and life, and of the unrighteous to annihilation.

## The Doctrine of Salvation

To begin, it is interesting to note that Jesus alone, of all humans, has so far been saved![21]

A. "Salvation is by faith in Jesus Christ by which one is enabled to keep the Law. Acceptance of Christ cleanses from past sins, but justification will be given only on condition that the Law is kept."[22] Thus it is that salvation is a process. And it promises no certainty until the resurrection. One who is born of God is "merely begotten spir-

18. Herbert W. Armstrong, *How You Can Be Imbued with the Power of God* (Pasadena, Calif.: Ambassador College Press), p. 5.
19. Ibid., p. 4.
20. Benware, p. 102.
21. Herbert W. Armstrong, *Why Were You Born?* (Pasadena, Calif.: Ambassador College Press, 1957), p. 11.
22. Herbert W. Armstrong, *What Kind of Faith Is Required for Salvation?* (Pasadena, Calif.: Ambassador College Press, 1952).

itually." He is "not yet really born." Only those who develop spiritually "shall finally be given immortality—finally changed from mortal to immortal at the time of the second coming of Christ."[23]

B. Baptism by immersion is an absolute essential. "There is no promise that anyone will receive the Holy Spirit until baptized in water."[24]

C. The keeping of the Law includes:

1. *Sabbath observance.* "To break God's Holy Sabbath is sin, and the penalty is eternal death."[25]

2. *Annual feast days.* They are: the Passover, during which set time the Lord's Supper is observed; Seven Days of Unleavened Bread, which follow the Passover; Pentecost, which symbolizes the coming of the Holy Spirit; Feast of Trumpets; Day of Atonement (Yom Kippur), which pictures the future day when "the responsibility for sin will be placed on the head of Satan, the devil"—Satan is the scapegoat![26]

3. *The Ten Commandments.* The second commandment, relating to graven images, is interpreted as excluding all idolatrous church festivals, such as Christmas, Easter, New Year's Day, Lent, and so forth—even birthdays! The seventh commandment, "Thou shalt not commit adultery," means that only a first marriage is valid. Divorce is sinful, for whatever cause. Any marriage subsequent to divorce is adultery. However, it is understood that there has been a softening of the attitude of the Worldwide Church of God in this regard.

4. *Dietary regulations.* The dietary regulations of Leviticus 11 and Deuteronomy 14 are mandatory, as are the de-

---

23. Armstrong, *All About Water Baptism*, p. 2.
24. Ibid., p. 8.
25. Herbert W. Armstrong, *Which Day Is the Sabbath of the New Testament?* (Pasadena, Calif.: Ambassador College Press, 1952), p. 56.
26. K. C. Herrmann, *God's Sacred Calendar, 1970-71* (Pasadena, Calif.: Ambassador College Press, 1970), p. 11.

cisions of the Jerusalem Council of Acts 15. Smoking is a sin, but drinking alcoholic beverages is not.

(It might be noted here that "Sickness is only the penalty of physical transgression, and whenever one is sick, he is paying the penalty. Healing is nothing more or less than the forgiveness of sin. God is the only real physician! Scripture labels other modes of healing idolatry. Medicine has a pagan origin."[27] Armstrongism advocates the laying on of hands and anointing with oil for healing. Tongues-speaking is denounced as being of the devil.)

5. *Tithing.* Tithing is a major emphasis, with "free-will offerings." In practice, this includes a first tithe, second tithe, third tithe, and so on. Instances are quoted of members who give 30-40 percent of their income to the church.

D. However, "a majority of those who die without Christ will be resurrected and gain opportunity to believe during the Millennium."[28]

### The Doctrine of Things to Come

"According to Armstrong, the year 1972 should have ended the work of God and brought in the events of the last days (1934 to 1972 completes the two nineteen-year time cycles.) This has caused Armstong some prophetic problems."[29] Nevertheless, the introduction to lesson 4 of the Correspondence Course declares that "no other Bible course in this world even dares to reveal the future as does this Course; . . . this Work really understands Bible prophecy."[30]

A. We are now in the last days, which precede the Tribulation—the time of Satan's wrath. The Tribulation will last three and one-half years and will be followed by the

27. Herbert W. Armstrong, *Does God Heal Today?* (Pasadena, Calif.: Ambassador College Press, 1952), p. 8.
28. Herbert W. Armstrong, *Predestination—Does the Bible Teach It?* (Pasadena, Calif.: Radio Church of God, 1957).
29. Benware, p. 66.
30. Ambassador College Bible Correspondence Course, lesson 4.

time of God's wrath. This is the sixth seal of Revelation 6:12-13. During this time, apparently, the "faithful" will be supernaturally transported to Petra, the ancient rock-walled city on Edom. There they will be protected from the horrors going on in the world. The time of God's wrath is the beginning of the Day of the Lord, which climaxes in the second coming of Christ.

B. At the Battle of Armageddon, the hosts of wickedness will be destroyed by the returning Christ. At the same time, the first resurrection will take place. The "dead in Christ" will rise and, together with the "living," will be changed from mortal to immortal. After rising to meet the Lord, they will immediately descend with Him to rule over the millennial earth. Satan will be bound, and the 1,000 years of peace and prosperity will ensue.

C. The second resurrection will involve those who never really had a fair chance to hear the truth. This is the judgment of the great white throne. "Isa. 65:20 indicates those resurrected at that time will live for a hundred years."[31] The Gospel will be explained, but Satan "will be ... allowed freedom to deceive the nations again."[32] It is hoped that most will believe the truth and be converted. All who do not will be cast into the lake of fire.

D. The third resurrection follows immediately after the judgment of the great white throne. "This handful of recalcitrant sinners will be annihilated—cast into the Lake of Fire. The Father will then move his throne to earth, and the earth will become the eternal center of the universe."[33]

E. Heaven apparently is reserved for the Father and His angels.

31. Herbert W. Armstrong, *If You Die, Will You Live Again?* (Pasadena, Calif.: Ambassador College Press), p. 7.
32. Herbert W. Armstrong, *What Is Satan's Fate?* (Pasadena, Calif.: Ambassador College Press), p. 4.
33. Joseph Hopkins, *The Armstrong Empire* (Grand Rapids: Eerdmans, 1974), p. 97.

Christ will reign on earth throughout eternity.[34] "The
Earth, and a definite, specific location on the earth, will be
where Jesus said He is going to be. If we are to be with
Him where He is to be—then we, also, are going to be on
this earth."[35]

*Hell, sheol, hades,* and *the lake of fire* all appear to be
considered synonymous terms. "The wicked will be resurrected at the close of the Millennium, but only to be annihilated."[36] Acknowledging that Jesus spoke of "the fire
that never shall be quenched" (Mark 9:43), the Worldwide Church of God teaches that the fire "will burn itself
out, when the wicked and all their wicked works are
burned up."[37] Satan and his angels, however, being spirit
beings, "will be tormented unto the ages of ages. . . . The
exact nature of their eternal punishment is yet to be determined."[38]

34. Ibid.
35. Herbert W. Armstrong, *Will You Get to Heaven?* (Pasadena, Calif.:
    Ambassador College Press), p. 11.
36. Herbert W. Armstrong, *Lazarus and the Rich Man* (Pasadena: Ra-
    dio Church of God, 1953).
37. Herbert W. Armstrong, *What Is This Place Called Hell?* (Pasadena,
    Calif.: Ambassador College Press), p. 18.
38. Armstrong, *What Is Satan's Fate?*, p. 7.

# 5

## The Way International

"THE WAY INTERNATIONAL is a biblical research and teaching organization concerned with setting before men and women of all ages the inherent accuracy of the Word of God (the Bible) so that everyone who so desires may know the power of God in his life. The Way is not a church, nor is it a denomination or a religious sect of any sort."[1] This is the introductory declaration in an attractive, multicolored pamphlet entitled *This Is The Way*. Its terminology is essentially that of evangelical Christianity. It offers, reputedly for a fee of $100, study classes focusing on power for abundant living. Capitalizing on the discontent and enthusiasm of youth, The Way International purports to give new light on the Scriptures. This new light is the outcome of over thirty years of biblical research and teaching by its founder and president, Dr. Victor Paul Wierwille.

The Doctor, as he is called by his followers, studied at the University of Chicago and at Princeton Theological Seminary, where he was awarded the Master of Theology degree. His doctoral degree is from Pike's Peak Bible Seminary, a reputed degree mill. For sixteen years he served as a pastor in northwestern Ohio with the Evangelical and Reformed Church, later known as the United Church of Christ. He resigned his pastorate in Van Wert, Ohio, in 1957 to begin his present activity.

1. *This Is The Way* (New Knoxville, Ohio: The Way, Inc., International, n.d.).

The heart of his "new light" on the Scriptures is presented in four volumes which make up *Studies in Abundant Living*. The style is disparaging of much orthodox biblical interpretation. Dogmatic and critical, the Doctor is not slow to write that nothing is so dynamically thrilling as the inherent accuracy of God's wonderful, matchless Word, and to indicate that he has the only true interpretation. "The Word of God is the Will of God. It means what it says and says what it means."[2] And he, the Doctor, is the one who knows what it means!

"God," he testifies, "spoke to me audibly, just like I'm talking to you now. He said He would teach me the Word as it had not been known since the first century, if I would teach it to others."[3] God later give him a sign in confirmation of the voice. In response to his request, God sent snow. One moment the sky was crystal and clear. He closed his eyes. When he opened them, he testified, the "sky was so white and thick with snow I couldn't see the tanks at the filling station on the corner not 75 feet away."[4] He later received the "holy spirit," and spoke in tongues. "The holy spirit field—that's the field God raised me up for. . . . And there's no one I can't lead into speaking in tongues if they are Christian and want to do it."[5]

The Way International has been characterized as combining biblical literalism, evangelicalism, Calvinism, ultra-dispensationalism, and Pentecostalism.[6] Wierwille uses Scripture extensively to prove teaching that is far from orthodox. His use of Hebrew and Greek, with appropriate explanations, is impressive (as it is no doubt intended to be).

2. Victor Paul Wierwille, *The Word's Way*, Studies in Abundant Living, vol. 3 (New Knoxville, Ohio: American Christian Press, 1971), p. 229 (hereafter cited as WW).
3. Elena S. Whiteside, *The Way: Living in Love* (New Knoxville, Ohio: American Christian Press, 1972), p. 178.
4. Ibid., p. 180.
5. Ibid., p. 201.
6. J. M. Hopkins, "The Word and the Way According to V. Wierwille," *Christianity Today*, September 26, 1975, p. 42.

The Structure of The Way is likened to that of a tree. "Leaves and twigs, branches, limbs, trunk, and roots. Each statewide unit is a limb, each city unit a branch, each household fellowship group a twig, each believer a leaf."[7] The leaf becomes "rooted and grounded and established" in knowledge and practical application of the Word in the "twig."

## THE SOURCE OF AUTHORITY

The one and only recognized source of authority is the Bible. But it is the Bible as distinctively reinterpreted by the founder. A strong dispensational view indicates that the "church began with Paul's Epistles. The Gospels belong in the Old Testament; and only those New Testament Epistles addressed to the church apply to believers today— although the remainder of the Bible is 'for our learning.' "[8] *The Way Magazine* of September-October 1974 declares that "the Pauline epistles are absolutely flawless, divine revelation. . . . In the Gospels we do not see the ministry of the Lord Jesus Christ at the right hand of God. . . . The gospels give only a sense-knowledge acquaintance of the Lord Jesus Christ." Further, "the so-called Christian Church today is built essentially on man-made doctrine, tradition, confusion, bondage trips, and contradiction to the Word as it was originally 'God-breathed.' "[9]

## THE DOCTRINE OF GOD

Elohim, God alone, is Creator of heaven and earth. The Way, like the Jehovah's Witnesses, categorically rejects any suggestion of Trinitarian doctrine. Such teaching is relegated to religion that began in the time of Nimrod. The plural word *Elohim* (as in Gen. 1:1) is simply indicative of supremacy and lordship, the plural of majesty. (An

7. *This Is The Way.*
8. J. L. Williams, *Contemporary Cults (The Way)* (Burlington, N. C.: New Directions Evang. Assoc., n.d.), p. 8.
9. *The Way Magazine*, September-October 1974, pp. 3, 7.

interesting note on Genesis 1:28 states that the command
to replenish the earth indicates that prehistoric man ante-
dated Adam and Eve.)

## The Doctrine of Jesus Christ

A. Jesus Christ is not God. In 1975, Wierwille wrote a
book with this title. Enlarging upon material already published, it is a bold and acknowledged disagreement with
orthodox Trinitarian doctrine.

1. Jesus was not coexistent with God, either in spirit or
any other form. "God is eternal whereas Jesus was born.
Matthew 1:18" (WW 26). On the declared basis that God
was alone from the beginning, it follows that God is the
"Word" of John 1:1. This verse is interpretatively corrected to read: "In the beginning was the Word [God] and
the [revealed] Word was with God" (WW 28, brackets are
Wierwille's).

2. The created Word (Jesus Christ) was with God *in His
foreknowledge*. God, being spirit, had to find means to
manifest Himself "in concretion." He gave the revealed
Word so that man might be able to understand His communication. The revealed Word refers to both the written
Word (the Bible) and the created Word (Jesus Christ).
It is interesting to note that "we the chosen of God were
called in Him in His foreknowledge," in the same way that
Jesus Christ was with God "in His foreknowledge" (WW
29).

B. Jesus Christ was a perfect man. Wierwille adamantly
declares that Jesus is the "Son of God, but not God." "He
was a specially created, perfect man whose body came from
Mary and whose soul or 'life Principle'—manifested as
'blood'—was specially created by God in Mary's womb."[10]
Christ is presented as having been uniquely created by a
form of divine insemination so that He was born sinless.

10. Williams, p. 9.

"Jesus Christ's existence began when He was conceived by God's creating the soul-life of Jesus in Mary. God created, brought into existence, this life in an ovum in Mary's womb" (WW 37). John 1:13 is cited as proof of this. This verse refers, according to the Doctor, not to the believer, but to Christ. "He was born (begotten) NOT OF BLOOD. . . . The only one who did not partake as a natural man in the life of the flesh, which is in the blood, was Jesus Christ" (WW 37). In *Jesus Christ Is Not God*, Wierwille interprets Hebrews 2:14 as indicating that Jesus only "took part, not all" of Adam's flesh and blood. "The life of the flesh in the blood of Jesus came by way of supernatural conception by the Holy Spirit, God."[11]

Other Scriptures which demonstrate the deity of Christ are brushed aside by reinterpretation. John 10:30 reads "I and my Father are one." Wierwille holds that this means simply that they were "one in purpose." He makes no mention of the violent reaction of the Jews who heard the statement. They certainly took his meaning to be more than oneness of purpose! Hebrews 1:2 is taken to mean that the worlds were made *for* the Son, not by the Son. Likewise Ephesians 3:9, which is translated to read, "all things were created by (on account of, or for) Jesus Christ."

C. Wierwille maintains the dogmatic position that Christ was crucified on Wednesday and was raised seventy-two hours later on Saturday afternoon. This teaching is not unique. Numerous evangelicals concur with this view. The founder-director of The Way had further light, however, on the events of that day. He takes strong, and lengthy, exception to the teaching that Jesus actually carried the cross. There is "no record" of this, he says. The cross was borne all the way by Simon, the Cyrenian. "The unlearned man has made the cross of Jesus a wooden cross.

11. Victor Paul Wierwille, *Jesus Christ Is Not God* (New Knoxville, Ohio: American Christian Press, 1975), p. 71.

The Word says, and the spiritual man knows, that Christ's cross was sin, bondage, sickness, and pain. A wooden cross could not accomplish anything, but the cross of Jesus did much" (WW 227). A point incidental to this: "Wierwille concurs with the Witnesses and with Armstrong in the teaching that the victims died upon stakes rather than crosses."[12]

There were four men crucified with Christ—two thieves and two malefactors. This contention is largely based on the use of different words by Matthew and Luke. "The two malefactors (*duo kakourgoi:* [Luke 23:32-33]) were crucified at the time Jesus was crucified, while the two robbers (*duo lēstai* [Matt. 27:38]) were crucified later" (WW 240). Making considerable use of the niceties of New Testament Greek, Wierwille exalts his own ability to "read accurately and to study what is written."

Another notable rejection of accepted orthodox teaching changes the translation of the Aramaic words "Eli, Eli, lama sabachthani?" (Matt. 27:46). These words were uttered by Christ while on the cross, and are commonly rendered, "My God, my God, why hast thou forsaken me?" Wierwille's translation is "My God, my God, for this purpose was I spared, for this purpose was I kept, for this purpose came I into the world, for this purpose was I reserved" (WW 273). He makes no mention of Psalm 22:1, from which these words were actually quoted.

## THE DOCTRINE OF REDEMPTION

A. Redemption is by faith in Jesus Christ. Any Jew or Gentile who confesses Jesus Christ as his Lord and believes that God raised Him from the dead is born again and is a member of the body of Christ. "He has Christ in him, the hope of glory." This will be recognized as evangelical truth. It must, of course, be tempered by the realization

12. Hopkins, p. 40.

that the essential deity of Christ is denied. And without the deity of Christ, there is no adequate atonement.

In *Jesus Christ Is Not God*, Wierwille felt it necessary to fulminate on this point. "Trinitarian dogma," he writes, "degrades God from his elevated, unparalleled position; besides, it leaves man unredeemed."[13] Further, "if Jesus Christ is God and not the Son of God, we have not yet been redeemed."[14] In this, the founder of The Way rejects the truth that Jesus Christ is the God-man, the perfect sacrifice and perfect substitute for sinful man.

B. Salvation includes deliverance from the power of darkness. That is, "when we have salvation, we have wholeness, even physical wholeness if we simply accept it."[15] Complete healing from any sickness or disability is available to all believers. Apparently this is not a matter of extreme emphasis. When asked to tell of "some fantastic healings," the Doctor answered, "I don't remember too many specific healings. You see . . . healings and miracles are a result of the Word of God living in a person's heart . . . by-products of the Word."[16]

C. Wierwille differentiates between the bride of Christ and the body of Christ. "The kingdom of heaven period is for the called-out (ekklesia) of Israel, the church of Israel, which is the bride of Christ" (NDC 7). This is the church of the period of Law and of the gospels. It will also be the church of the book of the Revelation, at which time the bride and groom will be together. On the other hand, the body of Christ began on the Day of Pentecost and continues until the return of Christ. During that period, "every one who is born again by God's Spirit is a member of the Church of Grace, the body of Christ" (NDC 10). Al-

13. Wierwille, *Jesus Christ Is Not God*, p. 85.
14. Ibid., p. 6.
15. Victor Paul Wierwille, *The New, Dynamic Church*, Studies in Abundant Living, vol. 2 (New Knoxville, Ohio: American Christian Press, 1971), p. 31 (hereafter cited as NDC).
16. Whiteside, p. 169.

so called the Church of God, it includes both Jewish and
Gentile believers.

### The Doctrine of the Holy Spirit and of "holy spirit"

Wierwille distinguishes these terms, with vehemence.
His contention is that God *is* Holy Spirit. (This, of course,
accords with his anti-Trinitarian position.) "And since
God is Holy Spirit, He can only give what He is—holy
spirit" (NDC 103). Whenever God the giver is referred
to as the Holy Spirit, Holy Spirit is always capitalized.
His gift, holy spirit, is not.

A. An individual receives holy spirit when he is saved.
This gift of holy spirit has nine parts, or manifestations,
as listed in 1 Corinthians 12. All of them are received by
all believers, including the gift of speaking in tongues.

B. "There's no one I can't lead into speaking in tongues,
if they are Christian and want to do it."[17] In pursuance of
the conviction that "the holy spirit field" is one distinctive
for which God has raised him up, Wierwille urges every
believer to exercise this gift. The experience of so doing
is the "overflow" of the spirit, and it edifies the body of
believers.

Speaking in tongues may be both in private and in public. In the first case, it is for prayer and praise, and is never
interpreted. In the second, it is for edification, and must
be interpreted. Apparently it is not uncommon for a period
of such "manifestation" to be programmed into public
meetings. An individual might pray by request, or by demand. It is emphasized that "what you say when you speak
in tongues is God's business, but that you *do* speak is your
responsibility" (NDC 109). Instructions are precise and
clear. "I am ministering the holy spirit to you. . . . Close
your eyes and sit quietly" (NDC 122). "Believe to be natu-

17. Ibid, p. 201.

ral and at ease. You have to move your lips, your throat, your tongue; you push the air through your voice box to make the sounds" (NDC 117-18). "Just breathe in. Open your mouth wide. While you are breathing in, thank God for having filled you with the fullness of the power of His holy spirit. . . . Speak forth. When you have finished one sound, speak another. Do not pay any attention to what you are thinking. . . . You formulate the words . . . You are magnifying God no matter what the words sound like to your ears. It is your part to speak in tongues; it is God's part to give the utterance" (NDC 123).

### CONCLUSION

Wierwille's writings are voluminous, and they are characterized by a personally distinctive exposition of Scripture. His writing style is extremely dogmatic, with interpretations that are frequently at odds with orthodoxy. A typical expression is "It simply isn't so," with reference to commonly accepted teaching. Not all his views are heretical by orthodox standards. While Christ's deity is denied, His birth, miracles, death, resurrection, and ascension are accepted as biblical truth. Regeneration is considered essential, and that by faith in Jesus Christ, God's Son. Eternal life, received at the moment of faith in Christ, can never be lost.

Wierwille's major emphasis upon "Power for Abundant Living" carries acceptability by many in this day of lowering standards of Christian holiness. He has applied Christian teaching to the whole man in all of life. Apparently this makes an appeal to many unsatisfied young people and others who are dissatisfied with the lifelessness of many churches.

# 6

## Hinduism-based Movements

THE INVASION OF THE WESTERN HEMISPHERE by Eastern mysticism is not new. Literary men have thought that New England transcendentalism of the nineteenth century was influenced by Hinduistic philosophy. Christian Science and Theosophy are basically Hindu in essential teaching. However, the primary impact, as Hinduism, was probably made in the United States at the Parliament of World Religions, in 1893. The news media expressed admiration for the brillance of the Swami Vivekananda, the representative of Hinduism. Heeding the pleas of many who heard him, he conducted a number of seminars throughout the land. As a result, the teaching of the Vedanta was established at several urban centers. Vedanta (meaning the "end" or "ultimate" in knowledge) is expounded in the Hindu scriptures called the Vedas. The teaching emanates principally from the Upanishads (c. 600 B.C.), supplemented by the Bhagavad Gita (Song Celestial, c. first century of the Christian era). The word *Upanishads* has various meanings, but carries the connotation of "secret doctrine," or "that which dispels darkness or ignorance completely."[1] The understanding is that those who attain Knowledge are emancipated from the bondage and darkness of ignorance. Having become one with the divine (Brahman), they will no longer be subjected to the pangs of reincarnation.

1. Charles Samuel Braden, *The Scriptures of Mankind: An Introduction* (New York: Macmillan, 1952), p. 111.

It is fascinating to note that the main concern of the ancients was to explain how man relates to ultimate reality. Their solution lay in the realization that common man is ignorant of his own true nature. "Not moral transgression but mental error is the root of human misery and evil."[2] As non-dualistic Vedanta explains it:

> Brahman (the ultimate Reality behind the phenomenal universe) is "one without a second." Brahman . . . is consciousness. Brahman . . . is existence. Brahman is the . . . Eternal Nature of every human being, creature, and object. . . . Life has no other purpose than this—that we shall learn to know ourselves for what we really are.[3]

In the Upanishads the repeated declaration is, "That art thou!" The ultimate and infinite Reality, and you, are one and the same!

This is the teaching called monism, the "great discovery" of India's sages. It maintains that the superficial ego-personality which claims individual existence is unreal and transient. The fundamental principle is that man, in his real nature, is divine; and the purpose of human existence is the realization of this divinity within oneself. This is also called the perennial philosophy; it is claimed to be the eternal religion, the highest common factor of all religions. The goal, then, is God-realization, which is really self-realization. *Enlightenment* is a synonymous term. While it is a mystical experience, it is essentially experiential—it radically changes one's life-style now, and it also determines the eternal future.

This teaching is enhanced in the Bhagavad-Gita, the Song Celestial of the Lord Krishna. Three facets are basic: First, the soul of man is immortal, a part of the beginningless and endless creation. "There never was a time when I did not exist, nor you, nor any of these kings, nor is there

2. John B. Noss, *Man's Religions* (New York: Macmillan, 1956), p. 229.
3. Christopher Isherwood, ed., *Vedanta for Modern Man* (New York: Collier, 1962), p. 9.

any future in which we shall cease to be."[4] Second, the soul, or man, is eternally a part of the Infinite, the Absolute, the Brahman, the only Reality. Third, reincarnation (transmigration) and karma (the law of the deed, the law of cause and effect) explain life as man sees it. Successive reincarnations (reputedly averaging 8,400,000) are the steps by which the individual soul climbs upward to become *one* with the Infinite. It is then freed from the "illusion" of individuality and enters into its rightful position of eternal life, infinite wisdom, and abiding happiness.

"Vedanta has one great peculiarity: it declares that there must be no attempt to force mankind to travel one path; but that we must allow infinite variation in religious thought, knowing that the goal is the same."[5] Thus wrote Swami Prabhavananda in *Vedanta for Modern Man*. It will be noted later that several of the modern movements tend to claim uniqueness in being "the only way," or having the "authentic technique." This is not in keeping with the historic teaching of the Vedanta.

A commonly accepted doctrine within the Hindu system is that the "teaching" (whatever its emphasis might be) has been transmitted through the ages by men who have "realized deity." Each of these, usually designated "guru" (teacher) or "Guru Dev" (Divine Teacher), taught his chosen disciples. At times the light would seem dim, but it would constantly reappear in and through one of these "great souls." Names such as Shankaracharya (the great exponent of non-dualism), Ramanuja (the great exponent of modified non-dualism), or Madhavacharya (the great exponent of dualism, which holds that men are separate individual personalities even after liberation) are well known to students of the Vedanta. The "gurus" of today consistently refer to their teachers from whom they re-

4. Swami; Prabhavananda and Christopher Isherwood, trans., *Bhagavad-Gita: Song of God* (New York: Mentor Classic, 1951), p. 36.
5. Isherwood, *Vedanta for Modern Man*, p. 30.

ceived enlightenment. Thus the Guru Maharaj Ji acknowledges his father, Shri Hans Ji Maharaj, as his Satguru; Guru
Maharishi Mahesh Yogi learned the technique of transcendental meditation (TM) from his teacher, Guru Dev; His
Divine Grace A. C. Bhaktivedanta Swami Prabhupada
teaches the supremacy of the Lord Krishna, as he learned
from his guru, Bhakti Siddhanta Sarasvati; and so on. None
of the present "swamis" claims originality, although each
indicates that his is *the* way for the present time.

Of the currently active "gurus," the young Maharaj Ji is
blatantly hailed as "Lord of the Universe," the "greatest
incarnation of God that ever trod the face of this planet."
Among a number of parodies on Bible verses, the one relating to Matthew 6:33 reads, "First of all one should have
Knowledge from Guru Maharaj Ji and afterwards all the
accessories will be added to him."[6] However, His Divine
Grace, A. C. Bhaktivedanta Swami Prabhupada, of Iskcon,
is presented as "one who knows the Absolute Truth." He
is to be honored as highly as the Supreme and Mighty Lord,
for "he is the great God's most confidential servitor." This
is frequently emphasized in the movement's publication,
*Back to Godhead.*

"The Upanishads preach that the best way of purifying
the heart is through contemplation and meditation, . . . an
unbroken stream of thought focused on an object."[7] Thus,
meditation is a common facet of Hindu systems. And the
mantra is likewise central in the practice of meditation.
Webster defines it as "a verbal spell, ritualistic incantation,
or mystical formula used devotionally in popular Hinduism
or Buddhism." It may be individually assigned by a teacher, as in TM; or all devotees may use the same mantra, as
in Iskcon. But the purpose is to "still the mind," to attain

6. Charles Cameron, ed., *Who Is Guru Maharaj Ji?* (New York: Bantam, 1973), p. 277.
7. Isherwood, *Vedanta for Modern Man*, p. 294.

perfect calmness. Such is preliminary to the ultimate state of "spiritual reality."

There is no suggestion of atonement for sin. Sin is more the absence of good, and it is offset by one's own devotion to his chosen path to salvation. At any rate, the outworking of the law of karma is absolutely inexorable. Good will be rewarded; nongood will be punished. Since Christ is generally hailed as one of the great divine gurus of the past, it is claimed that one may accept the present guru without rejecting Christ. They are really teaching the same truth, according to the Vedantic view. As the Maharishi observes, "the crest of Vedic wisdom . . . is the essence of Christianity, essence of Buddhism, essence of Islam, essence of any life."[8]

### TRANSCENDENTAL MEDITATION

Transcendental Meditation (TM) is undoubtedly the most insidious of current movements. Defined as "a path to God" by its founder and leader, it is propagated as "nonreligious." As such, it is fostered by several state governments, and financed by public funds. "The Vedas [Hindu Scriptures] provide a direct technique to cognize . . . that all-pervading reality, almighty God" (M 21). That technique is TM. "Just learn to meditate; go within and experience the Divine Nature" (M 158). But, having thus declared his message and purpose, the astute founder recognized that the religious message is not attractive to many in the sophisticated West. So he capitalized on a statement from the popular Hindu scripture called the Bhagavad-Gita. There the Lord Krishna says, "Let not him who knows the whole disturb the ignorant who knows only a part." Therefore, TM meets the ignorant on the level of his ignorance. "Very few souls are there in the world of today who would go for God alone" (M 169).

8. Maharishi Mahesh Yogi, *Meditations of Maharishi Mahesh Yogi* (New York: Bantam, 1973), p. 66 (hereafter cited as M).

TM's appeal is the claim to improve the quality of life; to develop the full potential of mind and body; to enjoy fulfillment of life. According to the Maharishi, man is already divine. He needs no savior.

Maharishi Mahesh Yogi graduated from Allahabad University, in India, and subsequently studied for thirteen years with his "swami," Guru Dev (Divine Teacher). The Yogi (meaning that he has attained union with the divine) began his movement in the United States in 1959. As of 1976, TM claimed to have more than half a million Americans who were trained in its technique, more than two hundred SIMS (Student's International Meditation Society) centers in the United States, one thousand chapters on college campuses, five thousand instructors in the United States and Canada, and twenty thousand new trainees every month. More recent figures indicate a decline, perhaps occasioned by a number of law suits which challenge TM's nonreligious status. The Society of Creative Intelligence (SCI) is the theoretical aspect of TM. The SIMS is the banner under which TM gains access to schools and colleges. The Spiritual Regeneration Movement (SRM) is perhaps the most evidently truthful of TM's subtitles. The Maharishi does say that TM "meets man on the level of man and transforms him to the Divine" (M 91-92). Maharishi International University, established in 1974 in Fairfield, Iowa, integrated the teaching of SCI into its four-year degree program.

The key to this technique of meditation is the mantra. By means of the individually assigned mantra, the mind of the practicer is drawn to the "deepest and most refined level of thinking." That is the "divine nature" which is in every man. The realization of this innate divinity automatically brings freedom from any oppression of guilt or from depression caused by the "darkness of ignorance." Surely there is no less demanding, easier way to supreme bliss!

(See M 90-93.) In TM, a mantra is simply *a group of sounds*. The effectiveness is in the sounds themselves. The mantra is usually short, and it is to be repeated silently over and over again as the meditator sits in a comfortable position with eyes closed. This he is to do for fifteen to twenty minutes twice daily. By it, his mind is "drawn towards its subtler stages until it reaches its own essential nature" (M 183). Incidentally, the mantra must never be spoken aloud or revealed to any one, else it will lose its effectiveness.

How does one receive his own personal mantra? The process usually begins with one or two free lectures. The trained instructor pointedly declares that TM is nonreligious. It is *not* contemplation or concentration. It is not a spiritual or philosophical experience. It is simply a technique for deep rest and relaxation. It does not involve withdrawal from life. Upon payment of a required fee ($55 for high school students, $65 for college students, $125 for working adults) the initiate receives instruction. During each of these private sessions, the instructor analyzes "the quality of energy impulses of the individual . . . and selects the mantra" (M 9). It is a "special sound whose vibration influences produce all good, congenial, favorable, valuable effects on the outer life" (M 184). The Maharishi underlines that the silent sound of the repeated mantra must "rightly correspond to the energy impulses of the man, . . . or it is sure to create unbalance in the harmony of the man's life. . . . This is the main strength of the Spiritual Regeneration Movement" (M 185-86).

After the instruction and analysis, and prior to receiving the personal mantra, the initiate *must* be present at a "puja" ceremony. *Puja* is the Hindi word commonly used in North India to indicate Hindu idol worship. (It is not used by Christians living in India.) Although the would-be mediator is told that he need not participate, he *must* attend. He must bring six flowers, three pieces of fruit, and a white

handkerchief, which are to be offered before the image of
Guru Dev. The ritual is conducted in Sanskrit, the ancient
language of India, the language in which the Hindu scriptures were written and which is used today as the Hindu
priests intone their mantras and their puja of the gods. The
trained TM instructor recites the required ritual, having
learned it by rote. "Even the physical movements which
accompany the recitation are choreographed in detail, and
carefully memorized."[9] But SIMS instructors are hesitant
to describe frankly the details of the ceremony to prospec-
tive mediators. The reasons are obvious.

The first of the three stages of the ritual begins with the
invocation "To Lord Narayana" and progresses through a
sequence of references to historical and legendary personages until it reaches Shri Guru Dev. He, of course, is the
immediate teacher of Maharishi, the founder of TM.

During the second stage, some seventeen items are of-
fered before the image of Guru Dev, the Divine Master.
Each offering is accompanied by the words "I bow down."
The flowers, fruit, and handkerchief brought by the initiate are individually placed upon the altar. The puja concludes with a hymn of praise and adoration to Shri Guru
Dev. He is addressed as "Guru in the glory of Brahma;
Guru in the glory of Vishnu; Guru in the glory of the great
Lord Shiva . . . to Him I bow down."[10] He is the one by
whom "the blinding darkness of ignorance has been re-
moved." Incidentally, Brahma, Vishnu, and Shiva make
up the supreme triad of the gods of Hinduism.

A former TM instructor wrote the following about his
experience: "At the end of the song, the teacher indicates
to the person to kneel for a few moments of silence, and
then, both still kneeling, the teacher repeats the mantra
selected for the person, and has him repeat it until he has

9. *An English Translation of Transcendental Meditation's Initiatory
Puja* (Berkeley, Calif.: Spiritual Counterfeits Project, n.d.), p. 1.
10. Ibid., p. 2.

it correctly pronounced, and then they are seated for further instruction. Many candidates I encountered while teaching TM objected to this religious aspect, but went along with it in order to learn the technique."[11] Another writer adds: "At the end of the puja, the teacher actually bows before the altar. Simultaneously, he makes a carefully rehearsed gesture towards the candidate which invites him to bow down beside his initiator."[12] Failure to comply disqualifies one from TM. During subsequent lessons, participants practice meditation, discuss their experiences in groups, and are then on their own.

It is claimed that the result is "a deep state of rest," "reduction of anxiety and emotional disturbances," "inner alertness," "reduced dullness and improved efficiency in perception and performance," and "more energy for purposeful activity."[13] The uniqueness of such claims has been disputed. It has been scientifically demonstrated that similar results ensue from other methods of meditation.

However, assuming that the practicer attains such results, is that all there is to TM? Pressed for an answer to this question, an instructor confessed, "The advanced TM meditator would find within himself a depth of power unimaginable." For TM is only a beginning, a gradual movement from matter to mind, and then to supermind. This final attainment is explained as being "union with the Divine," the "glorious Cosmic Consciousness," the realization of the self, which is the impersonal god who is in every man, being, and object. *This* is the purpose of TM. It is a subtle method of captivating the ignorant on the level of his ignorance. It offers peace without a Savior. No need of such, for the source of power is within. This do-it-your-

11. David Haddon, *Transcendental Meditation: A Christian View* (Downers Grove, Ill.: InterVarsity, 1975), pp. 9-10.
12. Myra Dye, "The Transcendental Flimflam," *Moody Monthly*, January 1975, p. 34.
13. *Scientific Research on T.M.* (Los Angeles: Maharishi International University Press, 1972), pp. 1, 3, 6, 7, 9.

self formula has greater appeal than the message of repentance from sin and faith in God's Son.

The Maharishi's planned deception in presenting TM as nonreligious has enjoyed remarkable success. The number of trainees reached a peak of 40,000 a month in 1975. Federal grants have been given for the teaching of TM in public schools in California and in New Jersey. The house of representatives of the state of Illinois resolved that "all educational institutions be strongly encouraged to study . . . courses in TM and SCI." However, in 1976 a nationwide Coalition for Religious Integrity (spearheaded by the Spiritual Counterfeits Project of Berkeley, California) filed a federal lawsuit to stop classes in TM techniques in four New Jersey high schools. The suit was successful. *Christianity Today* reported that the ruling was that "the defendants have failed to raise the slightest doubt as to the facts or as to the religious nature of the teachings."[14]

TM monthly enrollments slid to a low of 4,000 in 1977. News media suggested that this may have led to a "new advance" in the program. Teaching is being offered which costs up to $5,000. It purports to give "the ability to walk through walls, . . . become invisible, . . . [or] hover in midair and fly around the room." It leads finally to "actual mastery of the sky, flying at will." One enrollee expressed the hope that he will "eventually walk through a wall," but the technique he wants most is omniscience and knowledge of other planets. This is not out of line with the fundamental teaching that the deity is actually within every man. A final word in the report indicates that no demonstrations have yet been given, and that reporters are notably skeptical.[15]

### GURU MAHARAJ JI AND THE DIVINE LIGHT MISSION

"I have not come to establish a new religion. I have

14. *Christianity Today*, November 1977, p. 56.
15. *Time*, August 8, 1977, p. 75.

come to reveal the truth."[16] With these words, the youthful guru places himself in succession with Jesus, who "gave Knowledge," and with Krishna, who "gave Knowledge." In the book entitled *Who Is Guru Maharaj Ji?*, printed in 1973, the Guru is presented as the incarnate Lord of the Universe, the Perfect One! He is "the greatest incarnation of God that ever trod the face of this planet" (GMJ 9). His father, it is claimed, was recognized by thousands of Indian devotees as Satguru, the one living master who reveals the ancient Knowledge of the inner self. Prior to his death, in 1966, he offered "full prostration to the Lotus Feet of his youngest son" (GMJ 11). Maharaj Ji was thus the chosen descendant of the Satguru, "crowned with the crown of Ram and Krishna . . . to take the Knowledge to the world" (GMJ 12).

The key word in the Guru's teaching is obviously *Knowledge*. That is, Knowledge by which we "can experience infinity within our own bodies" (GMJ 17). Apparently this is to approximate the ancient Hindu Gyan Marg, or Way of Knowledge. Some two thousand trained disciples, called "mahatmas," meaning "great souls," are able to transmit the "experience" to earnest seekers of truth. They teach four techniques of inner meditation known as "Light," "Music," "Nectar," and "the Word." A Knowledge session usually lasts about six hours, and "there's really something to see, hear, taste, and feel." First, "by the grace of Guru Maharaj Ji," the devotee sees Divine Light, the "sun which is within ourselves . . . brighter than the sun you see in the sky." The "third eye" is opened, and the divine light of creation is seen "inside his head." As the devotee meditates on this, he "become[s] one with God." It should be mentioned that the Guru equates God (Brahma) with per-

16. Charles Cameron, ed., *Who Is Guru Maharaj Ji?* (New York: Bantam, 1973), p. 13 (hereafter cited as GMJ).

fect and pure energy (GMJ 20-21). Second, "in the Knowledge session, we are shown how to turn our hearing sense inward to experience an actual music, the essence of every sound in the universe" (GMJ 21). Third, the Taste of Nectar, the River of Life, "is the 'ambrosia' or 'Fountain of Youth' explorers have traveled to find, not knowing it lay right inside them." "Advanced saints and yogis can live on nectar alone, as Jesus did during his forty days in the wilderness (GMJ 22). The fourth session deals with the Word, "the primordial vibration that underlies everything in existence." "In and of itself this one Word is the one reality, the illogical yet undeniable 'first cause' of the universe. The universe itself." "This is the Word. This is God" (GMJ 23).

Specific details concerning the receiving of "Knowledge" are not related. Instead, it is generally stated that it can only be experienced, not fully described. It is clear, however, that faith in the Divine Guru and dedication to him are requisite. The Knowledge can only be transmitted by touch. "If you can't get this Knowledge outside," declared the Guru, "come to me and I will give it to you" (GMJ 249). Devotees (called "premies," from the Hindi word *prem*, meaning "love") are advised to meditate upon the light, harmony, nectar, and holy Word in a quiet place for an hour in the evening and an hour in the morning. They are urged to continue to attend the nightly sessions held in any of the urban information centers and to spend time in service for others.

The Divine Light Mission movement experienced a continuing setback in 1975. The Guru's mother, reportedly disgusted with her son's "playboy" life-style, announced that she had ousted Maharaj Ji as leader of the movement and awarded the title to one of his brothers. In spite of very little publicity during recent years, the "mission's 1.2

million adherents throughout the world have remained
faithful to Maharaj Ji."[17]

## HARE KRISHNA

"Once I was searching, but now I search no longer. I
am completely satisfied with Krishna. By chanting the
names of God, and living a life free from lusts, I will eventually become part of God." This testimony of an attractive sari-clad American girl illustrates the teaching of
what is popularly called the Hare Krishna movement—the
International Society for Krishna Consciousness (ISKCON).
Chanting the names of God, especially the "Supreme Personality of the godhead, Lord Sri Krishna," is the way back
to "our original blissful life." *Back to Godhead,* the colorful
magazine of the Hare Krishna movement, proclaims an essential root connection with the Vedanta. It is "the only
magazine in the Western world to present the authorized
transcendental science of God-realization known only to
the saints of India's unbroken disciplic succession."[18]

This movement is an example of the ancient Hindu way
of devotion (the Bhakti Marg). According to it, one deity
or manifestation of god is chosen to be the sole object of
devotion or worship. Krishna is actually considered to be
one of nine incarnations of the god Vishnu the Preserver,
who is one of the members of Hinduism's great triad of
gods. However, in ISKCON it is taught that "Krishna is
the Supreme Personality of Godhead and the supreme authority on the Gita, and He initially delivered the Gita so
that all persons could reach the perfection of life and be
liberated from all suffering" (BG 36:2). It is further
claimed that "Krishna consciousness is the perfect process
for solving all the problems of life because it can at once
end our illusory separation from Krishna, the Supreme

17. *Newsweek,* March 8, 1976, p. 14.
18. *Back to Godhead,* no. 36, p. 2 (hereafter cited as BG, followed by the
    issue number and the page number—BG 36:2, for example).

Lord" (BG 47:1). Krishna is the essence of all existence, and "is present everywhere, even within the atom and within the heart of every living creature" (BG 47:1). Our eternal consciousness of Krishna is covered by a cloud of forgetfulness. This cloud is dissipated by the chanting of the Mahamantra (the great mantra). This mantra, used by all devotees, is:

> Hare Krishna, Hare Krishna,
> Krishna, Krishna, Hare, Hare,
> Hare Rama, Hare Rama
> Rama, Rama, Hare, Hare

All problems are solved simply by chanting Krishna.

This is the message of the movement. Singular and simple as it is, it is a method of self-purification by "ecstatic absorption in God-consciousness twenty-four hours a day." The chanting of the mantra will cleanse the heart of all "contaminated dust and garbage." "Chant Hare Krishna and be happy," is a recurring saying. The ultimate, of course, is to "become part of God," as the young lady quoted above indicates. This is "self-realization," the "re-establishment of our lost relationship with the Supreme Personality of Godhead" (BG 47:7). It should be noted that the name *Rama* chanted in the mantra indicates the god Rama of Hinduism. He is another of the incarnations (avatars) of the great god Vishnu. Apparently, apart from inclusion within the mantra itself he gets little attention from the Krishna devotees.

The founder and spiritual master of the movement is known as His Divine Grace A. C. Bhaktivedanta Swami Prabhupada, an awesome title by which he is always addressed. But he is "the representative of Krishna," a self-realized soul who "as all scriptures reveal, should be honored as highly as the Supreme and Almighty Lord, for he is the Great God's most confidential servitor" (BG 36:26).

The principal scripture of ISKCON is the Bhagavad-Gita, in which Krishna is the supreme authority and speaker. The Gita, most popular of Hindu scriptures today, is contained within the massive Mahabharata, an epic story of a great war in India's long history.

ISKCON is a variant of the usual Vedantic invasion of the West in that it reveres Srila Madhavacharya rather than the honored Shankaracharya. Shankaracharya advocated the advaita, nondual, monistic teaching. "Madhavacharya always stressed that God and man are separate individual personalities even after liberation, and thus his philosophy is known as dvaita, or dual" (BG 36:3). Nevertheless, ISKCON includes "absorption into God," or "becoming part of God," as the highest attainment in eternity. With reference to a Bhagavad-Gita class, it "is stated in The Nectar of Devotion: Persons who are impelled by pure devotional service in Krishna Consciousness and who therefore go to see the Deities of Vishnu in the temple will surely get relief from entering again into the prison house of a mother's womb" (BG 36:15). This is tantamount to a declaration that reincarnation is no longer necessary. One has become "part of God."

The personal lives of the Krishna disciples are examples of disciplined continence. Men shave their heads, except for the Hindu *chutiya*, the usually small tuft of hair toward the back of the head. Women wear the beautiful and modest Indian saris. Eating is strictly vegetarian, as in orthodox Hinduism. Food is always presented to the deities first, and, indeed, every activity is "for the Supreme Lord." Sex is voluntarily given up, except for the purpose of having children in marriage. The dedication to Krishna is total.

*Back to Godhead,* the title of the magazine of the movement, indicates the proud purpose. Above the magazine name, in the front cover of each issue, the basic philosophy is declared, "Godhead is light, nescience [ignorance] is darkness. Where there is Godhead there is no nescience." Chanting the name of Krishna dispels the ignorance and reinstates the soul in the deity.

The communal lives of these young devotees of this form of Bhakti-yoga are scrupulously regulated. At 3:30 A.M. on an average day, the students are awakened by the chanting of Hare Krishna. Each day is filled with activity. Notable are Sankirtan (public chanting of Hare Krishna), printing the literature written by the spiritual master, and worship of the deity in the temple. "By His mercy the Lord appears in the Deity form of stone or wood." These grotesque idols are "bathed and dressed and fed," every morning at 4:30, in ISKCON Boston (BG 36:14). The Sankirtan party usually continues the "ecstatic chanting" and distribution of literature some six or seven hours a day. This "distribution of Krishna consciousness to the living entities who have forgotten Krishna is a far greater service than the patchwork of material welfare work, altruism, etc." (BG 36:17). The ISKCON publications are the work of the founder; they are mostly translations with explanation of Hindu scriptures pertaining to Krishna. The format usually gives the text in Sanskrit, which is followed by the transliteration in roman letters. Synonyms are explained, the translation is given, and finally the "purport," or teaching, is given. The work is largely unintelligible to an average reader. Yet people are persuaded to buy, moved by the fervent sales talk of the devotees. The devotees have made themselves obnoxious in numerous public places by their methods of persuasion, often considered illegal.

The founder and spiritual master of the movement, Swami Prabhupada, died in 1978. His decease has not produced any notable change in the activities of the devotees. Hindu dress, however, has apparently given way to a more

casual Western style among those whose assigned duties
relate to meetings with the general public.

## OTHER HINDUISM-BASED MOVEMENTS

Propagated with less flamboyance are numerous other
Hinduism-based movements in the West. The Self-Realization Fellowship (SRF), founded by Swami Yogananda,
has international headquarters in India. It has its SRF centers in Europe and in the United States. Its message is essentially that of the others mentioned. True happiness is
offered as the disciple "learns the divine nature of his being." The SRF method is the Hindu Karma Marg, the
Way of Works. Concentration techniques are imparted
only on the pledge that information will not be given to
others.

The Vedanta Society is an arm of the RamaKrishna Mission. The one who organized this movement was Swami
Vivekananda, who made a great impact during the Parliament of World Religions in Chicago, in 1893. The Vedanta Society also has centers throughout the Western
world, with more than a dozen in the United States. Each
center is an independent, self-sustaining unit which is governed by its members, with a monk in charge. He usually
holds the traditional title of "swami." Literally meaning
"lord," the title indicates that he has undergone training
and has attained unto the enlightening experience which
is the ultimate in the Vedantic teaching. Generally, no ad-
vertising is done, although the notice of public meetings
will usually be found among weekend church notices in
cities where the Society operates. There will be classes on
the Upanishads and Bhagavad-Gita. The message of the
Vedanta Society is thoroughly in keeping with its name.
That is, the message is in keeping with books classified as
Vedic literature. Brahman is the only reality. Men are
caught in the illusion of ignorance. The Vedas give the

knowledge that will free the individual from bondage and release him into the Infinite.

Besides these, there are "swamis," "enlightened beings" who operate independently. Message and techniques are essentially the same, with variants that are always permissible in the Vedanta. Concentration, contemplation, and meditation with the focus within oneself: it is *there* that the *Power* lies. Go deeper and deeper into yourself; plumb the depths of your own inner being, from matter to mind, and then to supermind. Thus we reach union with the Divine. That, according to the mystical systems of the East, is Sat-Chit-Anand—Truth, Consciousness, and Bliss!

# 7

## *Scientology*

SCIENTOLOGY IS A TWENTIETH-CENTURY WESTERN method that aims to reach the goal sought by the sages of ancient India. The method is defined as "an exploration into Terra incognita, the human mind, that vast and hitherto unknown realm an inch back of our foreheads."[1]

Claiming some fifteen million members, Scientology is an outgrowth or development of a study called Dianetics, initiated by L. Ronald Hubbard. Dianetics means "discursive reasoning," or simply, "pertaining to reasoning." This definition immediately distinguishes the teaching as being built upon the reasoning of man to rectify his past, and to determine his future.

Hubbard's book *Dianetics, the Modern Science of Mental Health* was published in 1948. The author had been a leader or member of four anthropological expeditions among primitive peoples, an officer in the U.S. Navy in World War II, and a writer of imaginative science-fiction thrillers for popular magazines. As an advance upon his theory of Dianetics, he "elaborated a theory attributing mental aberrations to prenatal impressions, 'engrams' received by the embryo in the womb."[2]

Scientology purposes to uncover and eradicate prenatal problems, compulsions, and inhibitions that have accu-

1. Omar Garrison, *The Hidden Story of Scientology* (London: Arlington, 1914), p. 20.
2. Bryan Wilson, *Religious Sects* (New York: McGraw-Hill, 1970), p. 163.

mulated in the soul during past lives. Presumably, the result will be restoration of the individual to present-time full self-determination, and continued freedom from those problems in the future state.

A simple explanation of the Vedic, or Hindu, religious philosophy will clarify this thought. According to the ancient Vedic (Hindu) scriptures, the individual soul (called "droplet" by some) somehow became separated from the World Soul, the Infinite. In a succession of lives, or incarnations, this droplet strives for absorption back into the Infinite, the One Reality. In this age-long process, the inexorable law of karma demands that each good deed be rewarded and each wrong deed be punished (karma is called the Law of the Deed!). Thus, all the deeds (right or wrong) of previous lives are balanced by rewards or suffering in the present life, or in future lives.

Scientology emulates this Vedic philosophy, but seeks to short-cut the karmic process by reaching the original aberration (called an "engram"), which presumably initiated the whole process of incarnations and reincarnations. By dealing with the original wrong, the soul becomes "clear," free to go on to better things, with no harmful accretions to restrain or detain it.

This is tantamount to the enlightenment sought by the Hindu wise men of ancient India, or the world-saviors of Buddhism. The only new parts are the methodology and terminology. Further, the method of Scientology takes much less time, and is much less demanding than the ancient methods of asceticism and meditation. But it costs much more!

## THE METHOD OF SCIENTOLOGY
The one seeking freedom, the Seeker, is positioned opposite an Auditor. This Auditor, or Counselor, directs the Seeker back along "his personal track to contact and relive

the moments of emotion, pain, and unconscious thought
that were filed in the memory bank of his reactive mind."[3]
He probes back through the previous lives, as necessary,
to the basic engram that started the chain that binds the
Seeker's mind and prohibits self-appreciation and deter-
mination.

What's an "engram"? Webster defines it as "a lasting
trace left in an organism by psychic experience." Here are
some of the other most commonly used terms of Scientology.

*Analytical Mind:* the conscious, active mind that perceives
and reasons.

*Auditor:* the Scientology-trained private counselor.

*Clear:* one who is clear from problems, difficulties, and
engrams; one with no neuroses or illnesses.

*Dianetics:* the method of "pulling out engrams" from the
Reactive mind.

*E-Meter (Electro-psychometer):* a crude lie-detector;[4] a
"confessional aid in Scientology . . . two empty tin-cans
connected to a simple galvanometer. The Pre-Clear
grasps the cans, while the Auditor asks personal and
probing questions. . . . 'Have you done anything your
mother would be ashamed to find out?' "[5]

*Engram:* problems haunting the Reactive Mind; carry-
overs from past and prenatal experiences.

*Pre-Clear:* the beginning Scientologist; the Seeker.

*Reactive Mind:* the storehouse of unpleasant memories;
area where engrams are recorded and stored; the unconscious.

3. Garrison, p. 29.
4. The E-Meter is an electronic device used to measure resistance to
a flow of electrical current passing through it. The galvanometer
indicates the amount of resistance offered by a body connected
between the two electrodes attached to either side of the device.
It has indicative dials and a control panel—read and manipulated
by the auditor as he advises.
5. W. J. Peterson, *Those Curious New Cults* (New Canaan, Conn.:
Keats, 1973), p. 91.

Basic to the whole method of Scientology is the "Thetan" (a word coined from the Greek letter *theta*). This is the immortal spirit, which may have been in existence for 74 million years.

This idea savors of Gnostic *aeons* (eternal beings) and the Hindu doctrine of reincarnation. Bryan Wilson explains:

> A theory of reincarnation was added: in the human mind was an immortal element, a Thetan, the scientological equivalent of a transmigrating soul, which was also subject to engrams, not only from the experience of the individual that it occupied at a given time, but from all previous individuals in which it had resided. The therapeutic process . . . was now extended to the clearing of the engrams of earlier incarnations.[6]

According to procedure, the Pre-Clear meets with the assigned Auditor in a private counseling session. As they sit with an E-Meter between them, the Pre-Clear grasps the two tin cans that are attached to the galvanometer. As the Auditor asks questions, the reactions of the Pre-Clear are indicated on the dials of the E-Meter. The responses, as seen on the E-Meter, reveal the engrams. They may be prenatal, pertaining to previous lives. Hubbard's followers are encouraged to probe into previous existences for troublesome engrams. One investigator indicated that it may take as many as twenty hours for the Pre-Clear to begin the upward movement toward becoming a Clear.

When the engrams are revealed, identified, and presumably confessed, they are automatically erased. They no longer cling to the harassed Thetan. The process continues until the Pre-Clear has dealt with the basic engram. It may have been an incident occurring to the soul hundreds of years ago, the beginning of a binding chain that must be—and presumably is, now—broken.

6. Wilson, p. 164.

The Pre-Clear moves up through eight grades of clearness, until he is pronounced Clear. William Peterson writes that ⅟₅₀ of 1% who have attempted this have made it.[7] Scientologists claim measures of clearness that are apparently satisfying. The cost of all this is variously reported, but always very expensive. We will note this later.

## THEOLOGY OF SCIENTOLOGY

Theology, per se, is virtually nonexistent. Horton Davies writes, ". . . Despite its quasi-religious vocabulary, [Scientology] has no theology worthy of the name, and its use of such terms as 'spiritual' and 'infinity' as equal to 'God' and 'the church,' without reference to Jesus, the founder of the church, seems to be a verbal camouflage to escape taxation . . ."[8] In the change from Dianetics to Scientology, clerical terms and accoutrements were apparently added to provide a religious aura.

Their ministers are garbed in full clerical garb, wearing a large cross. According to W. J. Peterson,

> The Church of Scientology calls itself a "non-sectarian religious corporation." Services are conducted on Sundays, but . . . are "more of a pitch for Scientology than they are for God." . . . the Bible is seldom used.
>
> Scientology has its rituals for marriage, christenings, and funerals. None of these rituals include prayer or any reference to God.[9]

Peterson goes on to quote Ron Hubbard, the founder and director of Scientology: "While the eighth dynamic is called the "Infinity of God, the science of Scientology does not intrude into the Dynamic of the Supreme Being."[10]

7. Peterson, p. 92.
8. Horton Davies, *Christian Deviations,* 3d rev. (Philadelphia: Westminster, 1972), p. 109.
9. Peterson, p. 93.
10. Ibid., p. 94.

The profound influence of Eastern mysticism is readily observed. The teachings of Scientology contain references to previous existences, prenatal influences, and future lives. And the clearing of the engrams from previous lives relates too much to the Hindu doctrine of karma and reincarnation to be coincidental. These teachings are Vedantic in essence, if not in precise terms.

Man is declared to be basically good. He "indulges in evil behavior because of painful past experiences stored in the memory bank of his reactive mind (the subconscious), along with the Thetan's own record of experiences in former lives."[11] Sin, therefore, is not mentioned. Evil is acknowledged as the outcome of the engrams that have attached themselves to the continuing existence of the Thetan. There is no need for atonement.

Scientology's aim is to maximize one's confidence in himself, and to give the individual the assurance that he needs nothing, nor anyone else in order to accomplish his own desires. The power is within the Thetan, which needs only to be divested of the accretions that hold it back from total freedom. And that is possible through submission to the Auditor using the E-Meter.

### HISTORY AND ETHICS

The Founding Church of Scientology was established in June 1955, in Washington D. C., by L. Ron Hubbard. In subsequent years, lawsuits have been brought against Scientology by the governments of Australia and Great Britain, as well as the Food & Drug Administration and the Internal Revenue Service in the United States. The charges have centered on the words *fraud* and *fraudulent*. "Is the E-Meter an authentic medical device?" "Are Scientology's claims fraudulent?" "Is Scientology a legitimate religious organization, and therefore, tax-exempt?"

11. Garrison, p. 51.

Reportedly, the U.S. Internal Revenue Service was "dubious about a religious enterprise making so much profit, especially when they found that, in Washington D. C. alone, the Founding Church took in $756,962 (in one year) and that 90% of this money came from fees and and not donations."[12] "Annual gross income, mostly from 'counseling fees,' is estimated to be above $70 million."[13] Hubbard receives 10% of all fees collected by Scientology centers, and "spends much of his time in international waters, sailing the high seas in his 3,000-ton, 320-foot yacht, with its blue-uniformed crew of 200 sailors and students."[14]

Scientology teaches that there are eight dynamics of existence. The Pre-Clear (beginning Scientologist) would expect to go through these eight stages in order to become a Clear. The advancement would require a varying number of sessions for each of the stages, perhaps as many as twenty. The prices per session vary from $15 to $35—total cost might be between $7,000 and $20,000. The eight dynamics, or stages, are: (1) Self-dynamic, (2) Sexual, (3) Group, (4) Mankind, (5) Animal, (6) Universe, (7) Spiritual, and (8) Infinity, or God. This last dynamic, however, does not mean that the science of Scientology . . . intrudes into the Dynamic of the Supreme Being.

Scientology is totally self-centered. The Pre-Clear is devoted to his own present and eternal advance. The movement is only for those who can afford it—it has nothing to offer to the poor. As to its ethics, William Peterson comments, "In the Scientology code are such statements as 'Never fear to hurt another in a just cause,' and 'To punish to the fullest extent of my power anyone misusing or degrading Scientology to harmful ends.' "[15]

12. Davies, p. 109.
13. James C. Hefley, *The Youth Nappers* (Wheaton, Ill.: Victor, 1977), p. 117.
14. Peterson, p. 89.
15. Ibid., p. 95.

Scientology is the antithesis of Christianity. The apostle Paul wrote,

> He that spared not his own Son, but delivered him up for us all, how shall he not with him also freely give us all things?   [Romans 8:32]

The founder of Scientology is quoted as saying, "Man is caught in a high and complex labyrinth. To get out of it requires that he follow the closely taped path of Scientology"[16]—if he can afford it!

---

16. Ibid., p. 96.

# 8

## Christian Science

"IN THE YEAR 1866, I discovered the Christ Science or divine laws of Life, Truth, and Love, and named my discovery Christian Science. God had been graciously preparing me during many years for the reception of this final revelation."[1] The system therefore embodies a revelation for which Mrs. Mary Baker Eddy had been prepared. She claimed that her teachings and healings were definitely connected with those of Jesus of Nazareth and that her doctrine simply revealed the law by which He performed His healings. This law, until it was revealed to her, had been lost since the time of Christ. "Our Master . . . practiced Christian healing, . . . but he left no definite rule for demonstrating this Principle of healing and preventing disease. This rule remained to be discovered by Christian Science" (SH 147:24-29).

Mary Baker was born at Bow, New Hampshire, on July 16, 1821, into a devoutly religious family. Her poor health, which seems to have been a characteristic of her life, led to experiments with various types of healing. She experienced a good deal of unhappiness. Her first marriage (to George Glover) was a happy one, but it ended with the death of her husband a few months before their first child

---

1. Mary Baker Eddy, *Science and Health with Key to the Scriptures* (Boston: Trustees under the will of Mary Baker Eddy, first published in 1875), p. 107, lines 1-6 (hereafter cited as SH, followed by the page number and line number).

was born. In 1853 she married an "amorous dentist," Dr. Daniel Patterson. He was unfaithful, and she divorced him in 1866. In 1877 she became the wife of Asa Gilbert Eddy, "the first student publicly to announce himself a Christian Scientist."[2]

In the meantime her health continued poor, and in 1862 she resorted to a man named Phineas P. Quimby. He had been healing sicknesses reportedly without medicine. He called his system "the Science of Christ," and she apparently was convinced that he had rediscovered the methods of healing practiced by Christ. Later, however, she repudiated any indebtedness to Quimby, claiming "I won my way to absolute conclusions through divine revelation, reason, and demonstration. The revelation of Truth in the understanding came to me gradually and apparently through divine power" (SH 109:20-23).

This "discovery" came in February 1866, a short time after Quimby's death. She undertook a healing ministry and taught her system to pupils, each of whom paid a fee of $300. In 1875 she completed the book *Science and Health with Key to the Scriptures.* On August 23, 1879, the Church of Christ, Scientist, was incorporated in Boston. Its stated purpose was to "transact the business necessary to the worship of God."[3] However, the Christian Science *Church Manual* states that the purpose of the new church was "to commemorate the word and works of our Master, which should reinstate primitive Christianity and its lost element of healing."[4] Christian Science, like Mormonism, claims to be the true Christianity restored after many centuries.

2. Russell P. Spittler, *Cults and Isms* (Grand Rapids: Baker, 1962), p. 50.
3. Edwin F. Dakin, *Mrs. Eddy, the Biography of a Virginal Mind* (New York: Scribner's, 1930), p. 151.
4. The Christian Science *Church Manual*, 89th ed. (Boston: Allison V. Stewart, 1915), p. 17.

## SOURCES OF AUTHORITY

"As adherents of Truth, we take the inspired Word of the Bible as our sufficient guide to eternal Life" (SH 497: 3-4).

"In following these leadings of scientific revelation, the Bible was my only textbook. The Scriptures were illumined; reason and revelation were reconciled, and afterwards the truth of Christian Science was demonstrated. No human pen nor tongue taught me the Science contained in this book, *Science and Health;* and neither tongue nor pen can overthrow it" (SH 110:13-20).

The sources are two: the Holy Bible and *Science and Health.* The second, since it is the interpretation and explanation of the first, is the final authority. The true meaning of the Bible is known only through *Science and Health,* which is said to be the "voice of Truth to this age, and . . . [a book] uncontaminated by human hypotheses" (SH 456: 27-28; 457:1-2).

The Bible as we have it is unreliable, containing many mistakes, according to *Science and Health.* These mistakes are manifest "in the ancient versions." There are thirty thousand different readings in the Old Testament, and three hundred thousand in the New, so that "these facts show how a mortal and material sense stole into the divine record" (SH 139:15-19). In another place, Mrs. Eddy was reported as saying that "the material record of the Bible, . . . is no more important to our well-being than the history of Europe and America."[5]

The title of the second authority explains its contents. *Science and Health* is a volume of more than seven hundred pages. The chapters begin with random Scripture quotations, which give the author a springboard from which to leap into metaphysical thinking. *The Key to the*

5. Mary Baker Eddy, *Miscellaneous Writings, 1883-1896* (Boston: Allison V. Stewart, 1910), p. 170.

*Scriptures* begins on page 501, with excerpts from the first
and last books of the Bible. Sample readings are:

> Genesis 1:1—In the beginning God created the heaven
> and the earth.
> The infinite has no beginning. This word *beginning* is
> employed to signify *the only*,—that is, the eternal verity
> and unity of God and man, including the universe. The
> creative Principle—Life, Truth, and Love—is God. . . .
> This creation consists of the unfolding of spiritual ideas
> and their identities, which are embraced in the infinite
> Mind and forever reflected [SH 502:22–503:3].
> Genesis 1:6—And God said, Let there be a firmament in
> the midst of the waters. . . .
> Spiritual understanding, by which human conception,
> material sense, is separated from Truth, is the firmament
> [SH 505:4-8].
> Revelation 21:1—And I saw a new heaven and a new
> earth: for the first heaven and the first earth were passed
> away. . . .
> . . . St. John's corporeal sense of the heavens and earth
> had vanished, and in place of this false sense was the
> spiritual sense, the subjective state by which he could see
> the new heaven and the new earth, which involve the
> spiritual idea and consciousness of reality. . . . This is
> indeed a foretaste of absolute Christian Science [SH 573:
> 19-28].

The chapter entitled "Recapitulation" should be read as
an illustration of the ambiguity and contradiction that
totally encompasses this strange system which is much
more Hindu than it is Christian. The introductory para-
graph declares that "absolute Christian Science pervades
its statements, to elucidate scientific metaphysics" (SH
465:4-6).

Two fundamental "truths" must be *ever* in mind in any
study of Christian Science. Actually these "truths" invali-
date and render needless *any* discussion. All subsequent

study *must* relate to these absolutes. The first is this: "God is All-in-all" (SH 113:16). The second is this: "God, Spirit, being all, nothing is matter" (SH 113:17). In her *Miscellaneous Writings,* Mrs. Eddy wrote: "Here also is found the pith of the basal statement, the cardinal point in Christian Science, that matter and evil (including all inharmony, sin, disease, death) are *unreal.*"[6]

## ❋The Doctrine of God

"God is incorporeal, divine supreme, infinite Mind, Spirit, Soul, Principle, Life, Truth, Love" (SH 465:9-10).

"God is infinite, the only Life, substance, Spirit, or Soul, the only intelligence of the universe, including man" (SH 330:11).

A. The reasoning of the Christian Scientist is based on the dogmas that God is All-in-all, and is wholly good. It is repetitiously emphasized in *Science and Health* that God is all that *really is.* There is absolutely no other reality. Whatever is not God is unreal, unsubstantial, nonexistent, and the result of "mortal error." Since the majority of men do not share in the "revelation of Divine Science," they live in ignorance. This ignorance is notably seen in the "false" belief that there are other realities. Christian Science demands that men accept this concept of the allness of God in its absolute, extreme meaning. They must give up any claim or idea that there is any separateness or individuality. The individual must submerge his feeling of individuality in the determined realization that he is one with the All-in-all. When questions were raised in the attempt to bring this concept within reach of human understanding, they were either ignored or brushed aside as irrelevant. They were the outcome of the "error of mortal mind."

6. Ibid., p. 27.

When asked if God is a personal being, Mrs. Eddy answered by equivocation.

> In Christian Science we learn that God is definitely individual, and not a *person*, as that word is used by the best authorities, if our lexicographers are right in defining *person* as especially a finite *human being;* but God is personal if by *person* is meant infinite Spirit.[7]

She made no clear affirmation or denial of God's personality. It is impossible to secure an unqualified answer in simple language. For instance, it is written that "God is individual and personal." But the statement does not stop there. It continues, "in a scientific sense, but not in any anthropomorphic sense" (SH 336:32–337:1). What is a "scientific sense"? This is not explained. In addition, having denied that God is personal "in any anthropomorphic sense," Mrs. Eddy nevertheless spoke of God in anthropomorphic terms. God hears, sees, knows, and loves. Further, the use of the term "individuality," is not meant to imply that God has a form. God is "the infinite, and divine Principle of all being, the ever-present I AM, filling all space, including in itself all Mind, the one Father-Mother God."[8]

The concept of God is a very hazy one. A person who is included in and inseparable from all that is (although there is actually nothing that is apart from God) is beyond human comprehension. The impression given is that God is an impersonal being, if such is possible. The follower of Mrs. Eddy could not possibly have any concept of God as the creator who has a loving interest in His creation. The sustained denial of the existence of any material or physical creation eliminates any such possibility. The refusal to admit the actuality of sorrow or suffering obviates any partic-

7. Mary Baker Eddy, *Rudimental Divine Science* (Boston: The trustees under the will of Mary Baker Eddy, 1908), p. 2.
8. Ibid., pp. 3-4.

ular need for help from an outside source, even if such did exist.

The Trinity is repudiated in the statement: "The theory of three persons in one God (that is, a personal Trinity or Tri-unity) suggests polytheism, rather than the one ever-present I AM" (SH 256:9-11).

B. The claim that God is all that really is carries with it the obvious meaning that there is nothing else apart from Him. Therefore Mrs. Eddy defines matter as "made up of supposititious mortal mind-force" (SH 310:5). "The objects cognized by the physical senses have not the reality of substance" (SH 311:26-27). "Firmament" in Genesis 1:6 is really "spiritual understanding." The "dry land" of Genesis 1:10 illustrates "the absolute formations instituted by Mind" (SH 507:2). "Water" symbolizes the "elements of Mind" (SH 507:3). Creation consists of the unfolding of spiritual ideas and their identities" (SH 503:1-2).

This teaching that "oneness" is the essential principle of all being was prevalent in the ancient East. *Monism* is the word used to describe the discovery of this oneness by the sages of India, as taught in the Hindu scriptures, the Upanishads. This volume is very abstruse, and beyond comprehension to most readers. Although Mrs. Eddy made little mention of Hinduism in any of her writings, she did deny any connection or similarity between Christian Science and Theosophy or Spiritualism.[9] She refuted a charge of being pantheistic by writing that Christian Science "finds spirit neither in matter nor in the modes of mortal mind."[10] The denials indicated that questions were being asked concerning the apparent similarity between Christian Science and oriental mysticism. Charles Samuel Bra-

9. Mary Baker Eddy, *No and Yes* (Boston: Allison V. Stewart, for the trustees under the will of Mary Baker Eddy, 1910), p. 13.
10. Ibid., p. 15.

den, in his volume *These Also Believe,* sums it up by suggesting that:

> The closest approximation to the thought of Mrs. Eddy is to be found in the Hindu concept of the one Real, and the illusory character of all else. So, also, her fundamental denial of the reality of evil and suffering is an almost exact restatement of one phase of Hindu thought.[11]

### ✳THE DOCTRINE OF JESUS CHRIST

A. In Christian Science, Jesus and the Christ are not the same. "The advent of Jesus of Nazareth marked the first century of the Christian era, but the Christ is without beginning or end of days" (SH 333:16-18). Jesus is simply the "human man" (SH 473:15) who "demonstrated Christ" (SH 332:19), being "the son of a virgin" (SH 332:23). Christ, on the other hand, is "the ideal Truth" (SH 473: 10), the "divine idea" (SH 473:16), "the spiritual or true idea of God" (SH 347:14-15), the "divine message from God to men . . . incorporeal, spiritual,—yea, the divine image and likeness, . . . the Way, the Truth, and the Life" (SH 332:10-14), "without beginning of years or end of days," (SH 333:18), the "reflection of God" (SH 333:21).

The incongruity of this entire teaching is startling and puzzling when we recall that it is taught that neither birth nor death is real. "Can there be any birth or death for man, the spiritual image and likeness of God?" (SH 206:25-26).

In a lengthy and much qualified explanation of the difference between Jesus and the Christ, Mrs. Eddy wrote: "The invisible Christ was imperceptible to the so-called personal sense, whereas Jesus appeared as a bodily existence. This dual personality . . . continued until the Master's ascension, when the human, material concept, or Jesus, disappeared, while the spiritual self, or Christ, continues

---

11. Charles Samuel Braden, *These Also Believe* (New York: Macmillan, 1949), p. 189.

to exist in the eternal order of divine Science, taking away
the sins of the world, as the Christ has always done, even
before the human Jesus was incarnate to mortal eyes" (SH
334:10-20).

It is not explained how there could be a corporeal Jesus,
a "human, material concept," when nothing corporeal or
material really exists. Perhaps explanation is withheld as
impossible of understanding by those not enlightened,
whose minds are "befogged in error." It should be noted
that the Christ is eternal, is inseparable from the divine
Principle, and is called the "divine idea." The man Jesus
was simply the temporary vehicle through which the Christ
was demonstrated. The corporeal Jesus was not "one with
the Father, but . . . the spiritual idea, Christ, dwells forever in the bosom of the Father" (SH 334:3-5).

B. The virgin birth is intimated in the statement that
"Jesus was the son of a virgin" (SH 332:23). But the commonly held belief that God the Son thus became incarnate
through the body of the virgin could not be tenable to this
strange system which denies the reality of any matter.
"Mary's conception of him was spiritual" (SH 332:26-27).
She "conceived this idea of God, and gave to her ideal the
name of Jesus—that is, Joshua, or Saviour" (SH 29:17-18).
Jesus was "the offspring of Mary's self-conscious communion with God" (SH 29:32—30:1).

C. The glossary of *Science and Health* defines *death* as
"an illusion, the lie of life in matter, the unreal and untrue;
the opposite of life" (SH 584:9-10). Reference is made to
the illusion of the disciples of Jesus, who believed him to
be dead "while he was hidden in the sepulchre, whereas he
was alive" (SH 44:28-29). Bodily resurrection is dismissed
with the definition that resurrection is "spiritualization of
thought; a new and higher idea of immortality, or spiritual
existence; material belief yielding to spiritual understanding" (SH 593:9-11).

Mrs. Eddy acknowledged that Christ Jesus was the "Way-shower" (SH 497:15) and that "man is saved through Christ, through Truth, Life, and Love, as demonstrated by the Galilean prophet" (SH 497:16-18). His "crucifixion and resurrection served to uplift faith to understanding eternal Life" (SH 497:20-21). He did not die, however, although his disciples believed him to be dead. He was alive in the tomb, demonstrating the power of "Spirit" (SH 44:31) to overrule material sense. It was thus that he "fully and finally demonstrated divine Science" (SH 45:6-7).

It naturally follows that there was no bodily resurrection. The illusory concept is carried through, however, in that "our Master reappeared to his students," that is, "to their apprehension he rose from the grave,—on the third day of his ascending thought [?]" (SH 509:4-7). To add to the confusion, it is also stated that he showed himself to his disciples to prove to their "physical senses that his body was not changed" (SH 46:14-15). It was for this purpose that he caused Thomas to "examine the nail-prints and the spear-wound" (SH 46:18-19). "In his final demonstration, called the ascension, which closed the earthly record of Jesus, he rose above the physical knowledge of his disciples, and the material sense saw him no more" (SH 46:26-29).

It is impossible to equate Christian Science with biblical Christianity in reference to Jesus Christ, His birth, His life, His death, His person, the atonement, His resurrection, and His ascension. There is not a single facet of His person and work that has not been distorted or denied.

## ❋ THE DOCTRINE OF MAN

What is man? This question is treated at considerable length in the "Recapitulation" chapter of *Science and Health*. The answer begins:

Man is not matter; he is not made up of brain, blood, bones, and other material elements. . . . Man is made in the image and likeness of God. . . . Man is spiritual and perfect. . . . Man is idea, the image, of Love; he is not physique. He is the compound idea of God, including all right ideas; the generic term for all that reflects God's image and likeness; . . . man is the reflection of God, or Mind, and therefore is eternal [SH 475:6-18].

In view of this, it is declared that "man is incapable of sin, sickness, and death. The real man cannot depart from holiness, nor can God . . . engender the capacity or freedom to sin" (SH 475:28-31).

The follower of Mrs. Eddy who appears to be ill is exhorted never to say "I am sick." This is tantamount to saying that God is sick. He is to remind himself that he reflects God. "God is not sick. Therefore I am not sick." The practitioner emphasizes, "Man is the idea of God. The real *you* is that spiritual man. Know the truth! Know the truth! The truth will make you free." Free, that is, from the illusion of sin, sickness, and death.

Through all of this, there is a subtle indication that in dealing with "man," Mrs. Eddy was not writing about "men," or personal individual beings. She suddenly changes to the subject of "mortal beings," who are the "children of the wicked one, . . . which declares that man begins in dust or as a material embryo" (SH 476:2-4). Since the real man and God are inseparable, man is not mortal. It is not clear as to the relationship between man and mortals, for mortals are " 'conceived in sin and brought forth in iniquity' " (SH 476:16-17). This is strange language to one who denies both sin and iniquity. However, "mortals" are exhorted "earnestly [to] seek the spiritual status of man, which is outside of all material selfhood" (SH 476:21-22). This exhortation is embodied in the repeated command,

"Know the truth." The truth is that God is All-in-all, and that "you" are inseparable from God.

It would appear that part of the illusion of mortal mind lies in the concept of the individual soul. Any such idea of individuality is in opposition to the oft-repeated statement that God is All-in-all. The suggestion that "immortal" is contained in separate "mortals" would lead to the unthinkable conclusion that "Soul, or Spirit, is subdivided into spirits, or souls—alias gods."[12] What, therefore, is man? He is the "image and likeness of God, coexistent and coeternal with him . . . forever individual; . . . but what this individuality is, remains to be learned."[13] The only certainty is that the perfect man is not subject to birth or death. "Harmonious and immortal man has existed for ever, and is always beyond and above the mortal illusion of any life, . . . as existent in matter" (SH 302:15-18).

## ✳ THE DOCTRINE OF SALVATION

There is no doctrine of salvation within Christian Science, as the term *salvation* is commonly understood. In view of what has been written above, the question might be asked, Who is to be saved from what? Mrs. Eddy gave this definition of salvation: "Life, Truth, and Love understood and demonstrated as supreme over all; sin, sickness, and death destroyed" (SH 593:20-22). The basic fact concerning sin is that unrealities seem real to the erring belief of mortal minds. "Christ came to destroy the belief of sin" (SH 473:6-7).

But it is elsewhere declared that sin brings suffering, and that "they who sin must suffer" (SH 37:2-3). So the idea persists that the coming of Christ was somehow related to the illusion of sin. The *Christ* did make a spiritual offering. But it is emphasized that the "*material* blood of

12. Eddy, *No and Yes,* p. 26.
13. Ibid., p. 25.

*Jesus* was no more efficacious to cleanse from sin when it was shed upon 'the accursed tree,' than when it was flowing in his veins as he went daily about his Father's business" (SH 25:6-8, italics added).

The enigmas are obvious. If matter is nonexistent, and suffering and death are unreal, how could Jesus Christ have suffered on the cross? If sin, disease, and death are all unreal, how could it be that "every pang of repentance and suffering . . . will help us to understand Jesus' atonement for sin and aid its efficacy" (SH 19:17-19).

The great work of Jesus, however, was to teach "the way of Life by demonstration" (SH 25:13). He was essentially the Way-shower, and the efficacy of the crucifixion lay in the "practical affection and goodness it demonstrated for mankind" (SH 24:27-28). This is summed up in the fourth of the religious tenets of Christian Science.

> We acknowledge Jesus' atonement as the evidence of divine, efficacious Love, unfolding man's unity with God through Jesus Christ the Way-shower; and we acknowledge that man is saved through Christ, through Truth, Life, and Love as demonstrated by the Galilean Prophet in healing the sick and overcoming sin and death [SH 497:13-19].

## ✳ THE DOCTRINE OF THE FUTURE

Eschatology has little or no place in Christian Science. Heaven and hell are not places. Heaven is "harmony; the reign of Spirit; . . . the atmosphere of Soul" (SH 587:25-27). Hell is "mortal belief; error, lust; . . . suffering and self-destruction, self-imposed agony; effects of sin" (SH 588:1-3). When the apostle cried, "Now is the accepted time" (2 Cor. 6:2), he meant, "not that now men must prepare for a future-world salvation, or safety, but that now is the time in which to experience that salvation in spirit and in life" (SH 39:18-22). This means that "now is the time for so-called material pains and material pleasures to pass away, for both are unreal, because impossible in Science" (SH 39:22-24).

The declaration that man is "coexistent and coeternal with God" strongly implies preexistence. Mrs. Eddy reasoned that if man did not exist before the material organization began, he could not exist after the body disintegrated. "If we live after death and are immortal, we must have lived before birth" (SH 429:21-23). The actuality of death is not admitted, however. It is only "another phase of the dream that existence can be material" (SH 427:13-14). The body cannot die, because matter has no life to surrender" (SH 426:30-31).

The possibility of reincarnation is denied by Christian Science. But the suggestion of some sort of transmigration is undeniable in the statement that "mortal belief dies to live again in renewed forms, only to go out at last forever" (SH 556:10-12). Here is another statement that is difficult to comprehend. "Mortals waken from the dream of death with bodies usneen by those who think they bury the body" (SH 429:17).

The need for cleansing, or for some kind of purification, is indicated in that "mortals need not fancy that belief in the experience of death will awaken them to glorified being" (SH 291:9-11).

> If the change called *death* destroyed the belief in sin, sickness, and death, happiness would be won at the moment of dissolution, and be forever permanent; but this is not so. Perfection is gained only by perfection. They who are unrighteous shall be unrighteous still, until in divine Science Christ, Truth, removes all ignorance and sin [SH 290:16-22].

Progression and probation are necessary, and "universal salvation . . . is unattainable without them" (SH 291:12-

13). To complete the scheme and deal with the possibility of regression rather than progression, Mrs. Eddy wrote in another place, "If man should not progress after death, but should remain in error, he would be inevitably self-annihilated."[14]

Hindu philosophy based on monism, with its teaching of truth-realization, absorption into the Infinite, and freedom from the bondage of illusion and ignorance, seems to have found a revival under a new name, Christian Science.

14. Eddy, *Miscellaneous Writings*, p. 2.

# 9

## *Spiritualism*

SPIRITUALISM MAY BE DEFINED as "the science, philosophy, and religion of continuous life, based upon the demonstrated fact of communication, by means of mediumship, with those who live in the spirit world." That is, believers in Spiritualism, or Spiritism, as it is sometimes called, believe that the personality survives beyond death, and that the spirits of the departed can communicate with the living. This usually occurs by means of a living person called a "medium."

The "gospel of Spiritualism" (Spiritualists use that phrase frequently) is the eerie story of darkened rooms, ghostly appearances, and voices from the spirit world. Offering, as it does, to put a person in touch with "departed friends," this "gospel" commonly flourishes after historic times when loved ones have died, as during war.

This is not a new cult. Its roots are embedded in the early history of man. Death has always been a puzzle to the living, and all man-originated religions can be said to have emanated from the desire to solve that puzzle. Does death end all? That concept has been rejected by all cultures, universally, primitive and civilized. What, then, happens to the person whose body lies inanimate and lifeless?

J. K. Van Baalen, in his *The Chaos of Cults*, writes,

But we do find traces of spiritism among ancient Chinese, Hindus, Babylonians, and Egyptians. Spiritism can be traced through the Roman Empire, and the Europe of medieval times. Of the present-day religious delusions it is therefore the only one which existed in biblical times, and the Scriptures are anything but silent on it.[1]

Modern Spiritualists apparently regard the universe as pervaded with a master Spirit, whose laws of operation, if known and used, would secure healing and wholeness. Miracles may happen, but they are not interpreted as interventions in natural law, or changes therein. Rather, they are breakthroughs of a higher form of natural law, whose workings are not yet fully known, or are known only to a limited group of gifted people, such as mediums or practitioners.

*The Spiritualist Manual* indicates that, in 1948, "an intelligence was disclosed that was accepted as based on natural law and not miraculous or supernatural as heretofore had been accepted. This is a fact that distinguishes modern from ancient Spiritualism."[2] This is, of course, a tacit denial of the presence of an infinite God, or supernatural Being.

March 31, 1948, is the recognized date for the beginning of modern Spiritualism. Strange revelations were apparently made to Margaret and Kate Fox by means of mysterious noises and rappings. The girls were somewhere between six and fifteen years of age. The "raps" were said to be the attempted communications of one who called himself "Old Splitfoot" (one rap indicated a negative answer, two raps doubtful, and three raps positive). Margaret and Kate were pronounced to be mediums, acording to some. The girls reputedly admitted later that the unexplained noises had been "childish pranks."[3]

1. J. K. Van Baalen, *The Chaos of Cults*, rev. ed. (Grand Rapids: Eerdmans, 1962), p. 31.
2. *The Spiritualist Manual*, 9th rev. (Milwaukee: National Spiritualist Association of Churches, 1955), p. 74.
3. From *The Cults Exposed* (Chicago: Moody Correspondence School, 1962), p. 63 (and in numerous other sources).

In 1882, the Society for Physical Research was instituted by a group of sincere investigators. According to Horton Davies, "The proceedings of the Society in about sixty volumes constitute the most important record and evaluation of Spiritualist experiences."[4] Sir Arthur Conan Doyle, creator of Sherlock Holmes, was an avowed Spiritualist, as was Sir Oliver Lodge, the eminent British physicist. The late Bishop Pike of California gained much publicity for claiming that he had been able to communicate with his deceased son by means of a medium.

Belief in present-day Spiritualism is widespread. It is apparently much more prominent in countries outside of North America. *Time* magazine reported that Spiritualism was the fastest growing cult in Brazil, claiming some three thousand centers and ten million followers.[5] Current missionaries verify this, reporting that Spiritualism is rife in Europe, particularly in West Germany and France. It is reported that "every Sunday night a quarter of a million people in Britain attend meetings to receive messages from the spirits.[6] In the United States, membership appears small (a reputed 173,000 in 1965), but there are many who seek to consort with "departed loved ones" through numerous mediums. "It has been estimated that for every enrolled member there are ten or fifteen sympathizers. The United States census reports that the average attendance at every meeting is three times its membership."[7] C. S. Braden quotes a figure of 500,000 to 700,000 Spiritualists in the United States, and up to two million in the world.[8]

4. Horton Davies, *Christian Deviations*, 3d rev. (Philadelphia: Westminster, 1972), p. 69.
5. *Time*, 18 October 1954, p. 62.
6. Gordon R. Lewis, *Confronting the Cults* (Philadelphia: Presbyterian and Reformed, 1966), p. 164.
7. John H. Gerstner, *The Theology of the Major Sects* (Grand Rapids: Baker, 1969), p. 87.
8. C. S. Braden, *These Also Believe* (New York: Macmillan, 1949), p. 356.

WHAT DO SPIRITUALISTS BELIEVE?

Here is a Declaration of Principles issued by the National Spiritualist Association of Churches:

1. We believe in Infinite Intelligence.

2. We believe that the phenomena of Nature, both physical and spiritual, are the expression of Infinite Intelligence.

3. We affirm that correct understanding of such expressions and living in accordance therewith constitute true religion.

4. We affirm that the existence and personal identity of the individual continue after the change called death.

5. We affirm that communication with the so-called dead is a fact scientifically proven by the phenomena of Spiritualism.

6. We believe that the highest morality is contained in the Golden Rule . . .

7. We affirm the moral responsibility of the individual, and that he makes his own happiness or unhappiness as he obeys or disobeys Nature's physical or spiritual laws.

8. We affirm that the doorway to reformation is never closed against any human soul, here or hereafter.[9]

The influence of Eastern religions, particularly Hinduism, is readily discernible in several of these principles. Monism[10] and transmigration[11] are reflected in the first and seventh principles, and probably the eighth as well.

---

9. Quoted in Davies, p. 70.
10. *Monism* is the basic Hindu doctrine that there is only one ultimate reality; reality being one unitary, organic whole, with no independent parts. Any type of individualism, therefore, is illusion.
11. *Transmigration* is the doctrine that teaches that the soul passes, at or after death, to another body or succession of bodily forms, either human or animal. Each successive body is dependent upon the preceding life or lives.

### THE SOURCE OF AUTHORITY

In *The ABC of Spiritualism,* the National Association of Spiritualist Churches asks the question:

Is not Spiritualism based upon the Bible?

No. The Bible, so far as it is inspired and true, is based upon Mediumship, and, therefore, both Christianity (the simple and beautiful teachings of Jesus—real, primitive Christianity) and Spiritualism rest on the same basis. Spiritualism does not depend for its credentials and proofs upon any former revelation.[12]

The Declaration of Principles quoted above further affirms "that the Bible, so far as it is true and inspired, is based upon Mediumship and, therefore, both Christianity and Spiritualism rest on the same basis."[13] Thus, the Bible rests upon the Medium, not the reverse!

Gordon R. Lewis surmises,

The real basis of Spiritualism is not the Bible; it is the experience of the individual Spiritualists. For example, Christians believe in life after death as taught in the inspired Scripture. But Sir Oliver Lodge said, "I know that certain friends of mine who have died still exist, because I have talked with them!"[14]

Other writers, even believing Spiritualists, question the veracity or authenticity of the spirits from whom revelation comes. There are, in Spiritualist language, "naughty spirits," known as *poltergeists,* who are admittedly "playful" (or better, "deceitful"). Sir Arthur Conan Doyle testified that "there was no known test by which you could tell a bona fide spirit from a deceiver."[15]

A very weak foundation upon which to rest one's eternal state!

12. B. F. Austin, *The ABC of Spiritualism* (Milwaukee: National Spiritualist Association of Churches, n.d.), quoted in *The Cults Exposed,* p. 64.
13. Ibid.
14. Lewis, p. 165.
15. Ibid., p. 166.

## THE DOCTRINE OF GOD

As noted above, the first item in the National Spiritualist Association's Declaration of Principles states: "We believe in Infinite Intelligence." This is expanded by the statement "We express our belief in a supreme Impersonal Power, everywhere present, manifesting as life, through all forms of organized matter, called by some, God; by others, Spirit; and by Spiritualists, Infinite Intelligence."[16] This doctrine is a clear carry-over from the teachings of the oldest of the world's current religions, Hinduism. It is monism!

## THE DOCTRINE OF JESUS CHRIST

Spiritualists hold Jesus Christ in high regard. He is believed to be a truly historic character; admittedly, a miracle-worker, the world's great Teacher, and one to be followed. His deity is "most assuredly believed," but in the same sense that all men are seen as divine. *The ABC of Spiritualism* explains,

> Every man is divine in that he is a child of God, and inherits a spiritual (divine) nature. Just as a man develops his intellectual and spiritual nature and expresses it in life, he is "God manifest in the flesh." Since Jesus attained to and manifested in a very unusual degree the divine attributes of spirit, no spiritualist would question his deity.[17]

The deity, or divinity, of Jesus Christ is therefore both accepted and denied. If by the term *divine* one means "a member of the Trinity, co-equal with the Father (God)," then Jesus is not divine to the Spiritualists. If, however, the divinity means possessing a spiritual (divine) nature, as do all men, then, of course, He is divine.

Other Spiritualist references to Jesus Christ speak of Him as a "medium of the highest order," or, "an advanced

16. *The Spiritualist Manual*, p. 35.
17. B. F. Austin, Question 17, quoted in Lewis, p. 175.

spirit in the sixth sphere." He is also accepted as one of many Savior Christs, who, at different stages of the world's history, have come into the world to bring light in the darkness, and to point the way back to the "truth." He is one *Jagad-Guru*, World Teacher, among many. His virgin birth and bodily resurrection are brushed aside as "fables" or "myths." Any thought of vicarious atonement is untenable, because it is totally irrelevant, and therefore, unnecessary.

## MAN, SIN, AND REDEMPTION

Since all men are sons of God, progressing toward perfection in the spiritual realm by individual effort, Spiritualists see no need for redemption. Man is a god in "embryo," and the thought of a sinful nature, or indeed of sin itself, is abhorrent. Gordon Lewis quotes a Spiritualist writer, F. D. Warren, who ridicules the Garden of Eden story. Warren says,

> Man did not descend from Adam and Eve, but ascended through the natural evolutionary process from lower orders of animal life, and the Infinite Intelligence of Nature has decreed that man shall continue to ascend— the world without end.[18]

He goes on, ". . . there was no Garden of Eden, and no Adam and Eve, and no 'original sin.' "[19]

Thus, there never was a fall, and there is no sin. Evil originates in ignorance, which is dispelled as man climbs the ladder of evolution by his own self-effort to reach "heights sublime and glorious where God is Love, and Love is God."[20] "Man becomes a spirit after death, doing

18. Ibid., p. 180.
19. Ibid.
20. "What Spiritualism Is and Does," *The Spiritualist Manual*, quoted in Walter R. Martin, *The Kingdom of the Cults* (Grand Rapids: Zondervan, 1966), p. 209.

both evil and good, but he may be saved as he progresses from one spirit level up to the next."[21]

The Spiritualist author B. F. Austin exhorts,

> Believe in self. Know you are a god in embryo! This is the sublimest and most comforting fact in the world, giving assurance of man's individualized eternal existence. Eternal life begins when man begins to live in his divinity, the higher side of his character.[22]

And *The Spiritualist Manual* concludes,

> We do not believe in such places as Purgatory and Hell. Communicating spirits have merely graduated from this form of life into another. That life can be heaven or hell-like, just as each spirit chooses to make it; the same applies to our life here.[23]

### WHAT DOES THE BIBLE SAY?

God clearly instructed His people against Spiritualism and its followers. "The practice of sorcery was widespread in the surrounding ancient cultures, but Israel was prohibited from allowing sorcerers, spiritualists, mediums, or such like into their midst. . . . It was a crime punishable by death."[24]

The Scriptures are crystal clear:

Exodus 22:18: "Thou shalt not suffer a witch to live."

Leviticus 20:27: "A man also or woman that hath a familiar spirit, or that is a wizard, shall surely be put to death: they shall stone them with stones: their blood shall be upon them."

Deuteronomy 18:10-12: "There shall not be found among you any one that maketh his son or daughter to pass through fire, or that useth divination, or an observer of

21. Declaration of Principles (Milwaukee: National Spiritualist Association of Churches), No. 7-8.
22. Austin, p. 64.
23. *The Spiritualist Manual.*
24. John Rea, "Sorcerer, Sorcery," in *The Wycliffe Bible Encyclopedia*, ed. Charles F. Pfeiffer, Howard F. Vos, and John Rea (Chicago: Moody, 1975), 2:1613.

times, or an enchanter, or a witch, or a charmer, or a consulter with familiar spirits, or a wizard, or a necromancer, for all that do these things are an abomination to the LORD: and because of these abominations the LORD thy God doth drive them out from before thee."

Divination is defined as "the act or practice of foreseeing or foretelling future events or discovering hidden knowledge." It includes observing the times by the use of supernatural means, and is still common among non-Christian peoples. The mediator is called an enchanter, witch, medium, or shaman. The familiar spirit is a resident of the spirit world; through him contact is made with the "departed loved one" in the spirit world.

First Samuel 28:7-25 tells of King Saul's unfortunate encounter with the witch of Endor. First Chronicles 10:13 gives the finale: "Saul died for his transgression which he committed against the LORD, even against the word of the LORD, which he kept not, and also for asking counsel of one that had a familiar spirit [a medium], to inquire of it."

The apostle Paul met "a certain damsel possessed with a spirit of divination" in Philippi, and he dealt with her summarily "in the name of Jesus Christ," casting the spirit from her (Acts 16:16, 18). Earlier, on the island of Cyprus, Paul had rebuked "a certain sorcerer" (Acts 13:6), whom he called "child of the devil" and "enemy of righteousness" (Acts 13:10).

The clear and uniform testimony of the Word of God forbids any communication, or attempted communication, with "spirits," or any beings presumed to inhabit "another world" beyond the grave, or outside the ken of the physical world in which we live:

# 10

## *Other Current Movements*

A CHARACTERISTIC OF THE PRESENT DAY is the resurgence of the old religions of the world. Hinduism and Buddhism are awakening to make inroads into Occidental society. Various organizations in the West are actively propagating the teaching of the Hindu philosophy called Vedanta and spreading various shades of Buddhist doctrine. Baha'ism arose from a Muslim background but is notably eclectic in its sympathetic attitude toward all major religions. Other new systems have been created from segments of the old which have been transplanted into Christian settings, using Christian terminology. Most of these tend to syncretism. That is, they combine biblical teaching with other beliefs and practices. They do not claim to be Christian, and they uniformly dispense with any form of dogmatism. Common among them is the concept that "as all rivers lead to the ocean, so all roads ultimately lead to eternal peace." The best thing, according to many, is to choose the way that suits best and to work hard at it.

Of the current systems with some influence, several are notably Hindu in their major beliefs. This has been noted concerning Christian Science, which seems to have provided the impetus for similar groups. These deny or doubt the personality of God and impugn the reality of matter, sin, sickness, and death. Christ is a principle which is in all men, although seen in perfection in Jesus. Salvation is attained by the realization of the oneness of the individual

156

with the All-in-all. This is the At-one-ment! In most, re-incarnation is taught as the means by which all may have the opportunity to attain immortality as Jesus did.

## THEOSOPHY

THE NAME *Theosophy* is compounded from two Greek words, and means "knowledge of God," or "God-knowledge," or "divine wisdom." It denotes an eclectic philosophic-religious system which was founded in 1875 in New York. Admittedly derived from Hinduism, it does not claim any new concepts but presumes to present truths which are common to all religions. These beliefs form "in their entirety, the Wisdom-Religion, or the Universal Religion, the source from which all separate religions spring, the trunk of the Tree of Life from which they all branch forth."[1] It is maintained that the essence of all true religion is

> the knowledge of the One, whom knowing, all else is known, the knowledge of Him, that is the supreme, the highest knowledge. That is Theosophy. That is the knowledge of God which is eternal life.[2]

No member of the Theosophical Society is asked to believe or to preach theosophical teachings. He may profess whatever religion he pleases, since there is essential truth in all.

### THE DOCTRINE OF GOD

It is taught that God exists and that He is good. But it is the god of Hindu pantheism, or better, monism. Any thought of personality is untenable. Madame Blavatsky, first among the propagators of this revamped Hinduism, so declared: "We believe in a Universal Divine Principle, the

1. Annie Besant, *Theosophy* (London and Edinburgh: T. C. & E. C. Jack, Ltd., n.d.), p. 12.
2. Annie Besant, *Popular Lectures on Theosophy* (Chicago: Rajput Press, 1910), p. 4.

root of ALL, from which all proceeds, and within which all shall be absorbed at the end of the great cycle of Being."[3] This concept is amplified by Mrs. Besant, the other notable leader: "There is no grain of dust in which God's life is not immanent. . . . There is no other life than His; there is no other consciousness than His; there is no other Will than His. . . . There is only one life, one consciousness, and one power, and that is the life, consciousness and power of Ishvara (God), that are in all that He has emanated."[4] If one would know the hidden mystery, the divine Spirit, he is advised: "Find Him first in your own Self, and then you will see Him everywhere. . . . This is the Divine Wisdom, which we call Theosophy."[5]

### THE DOCTRINE OF JESUS CHRIST

Theosophy teaches about the hierarchy of supernatural beings who come in descending scale from the Lord of the World. These include the Adepts, or Mahatmas (Great Souls). They are the ultimate in human evolution, perfected men who choose to be reincarnated for the good of humanity.

The Lord of all these becomes incarnate from time to time as the Divine Teacher. He enters the body of one who is worthy. Jesus Christ was the fifth of these up to the present and is the master to whom the Christian should turn. Of course, it is recognized that there are other divine teachers in other faiths, worthy of the same worship of their own followers.

### THE DOCTRINE OF MAN

Man is an exceedingly complex being. He is called a "divine Fragment," and his ultimate destiny is absorption

3. H. P. Blavatsky, *The Key to Theosophy* (1889; reprint ed., Covina, Calif.: Theosophical University Press, 1946), p. 63.
4. In Charles Samuel Braden, *These Also Believe* (New York: Macmillan, 1949), p. 244.
5. Besant, *Popular Lectures on Theosophy*, p. 5.

in the impersonal god. Actually, man is " 'God' and not *a* god."[6] The true man is an emanation from the Logos, a spark of the divine. The human soul, in essence, is not to be distinguished from the Universal Soul. Man is said to have one spirit, three souls, one life principle, and two bodies, the physical and the astral.

Man is immortal. Death is merely the passage from one stage of being into another.

## The Doctrine of Salvation

Salvation is by the evolutionary passing of the soul into higher incarnations. Linked inseparably with this doctrine of reincarnation is the Hindu doctrine of Karma. This is the Law of Action and Re-action, expressed in the words, "As a man soweth, so also shall he reap." All good or evil committed produces fruit in this or in successive lives. The professed aim of life is an ordered progress through these incarnations until the ultimate goal of oneness with the divine is attained.

The individual can cooperate intelligently in his own evolution. "It is . . . part of this plan [the Divine scheme] for man's evolution that he himself should intelligently co-operate in it as soon as he has developed sufficient intelligence to grasp it."[7] There must be innate capacity plus earnest desire. Much time is necessary, plus self-sacrifice, abandonment of earthly ties and ambitions, and considerable self-discipline. The end is not easily reached. "As in the case of any other science, so in this science of the soul, full details are known only to those who devote their lives to its pursuit. The men who fully know—those who are called Adepts—have patiently developed within themselves the powers necessary for perfect observation."[8] "It has

6. Blavatsky, p. 67.
7. C. W. Leadbeater, *An Outline of Theosophy* (Chicago: Theosophical Book Concern, 1903), pp. 29-30.
8. Ibid., p. 9.

been proved," wrote Mrs. Besant, "and can ever be re-
proved, that thought, concentrating itself attentively on
any idea, builds that idea into the character of the thinker,
and a man may thus create in himself any desirable quality
by sustained and attentive thinking—meditation."[9]

The idea in mind is an ecstatic vision of the Ultimate,
of Unknowable, in which the distinction between the individual self and the Primal Being is obliterated. This is
Theosophy, or Divine Wisdom.

## THE UNITY SCHOOL OF CHRISTIANITY

THE NAME *Unity School of Christianity* is aptly chosen,
and it embodies the central principle of the organization:
"Unity of the soul with God, unity of all life, unity of all
religions, unity of the spirit, soul, and body; unity of all men
in the heart of truth."[1] The only right to the inclusion of
the words *of Christianity* is that Unity carries on its activity
within the realm of nominal Christianity. The organization claims no membership, and its adherents are members
of churches throughout the country. It was at one time
reckoned by one authority that "more than one-third of
denominationally identified Christians in the United States
have read or are reading Unity material."[2]

There is no one source of authority other than the writings of the organization. It is maintained that "Truth" is
not static, but ever increasing. Unity strives to interpret
the Bible, but it does not claim either infallibility or final-
ity.

The concept of God is impersonal. God is "Principle,
Law, Being, Mind, Spirit, All Good, omnipotent, omnis-

9. Besant, *Theosophy*, pp. 56-57.
1. Marcus Bach, *They Have Found a Faith* (Indianapolis: Bobbs-
Merrill, 1946), p. 223.
2. Russell P. Spittler, *Cults and Isms* (Grand Rapids: Baker, 1962), p.
73.

cient, unchangeable, Creator, Father, Cause and Source of all that is."[3]

Unity's aim is to bring about the realization of the oneness, or unity, of the individual with God, with infinite, omnipotent Being. The founder, Charles Fillmore, wrote: "Drop from your minds the belief that God is in any way separated from you, that He occupies form or space outside of you, or that He can be manifested to your consciousness in any way except through your own soul."[4]

The Unity concept of Jesus Christ sounds like that of Theosophy. Like Gnosticism, Unity denies the complete and absolute deity of Jesus Christ. He was a perfected soul who attained creative power in a cosmic evolution previous to human history. Jesus and the Christ, however, are not the same. They are separate entities who occupied the same body for a time. Jesus was a man, as we are. Christ is the cosmic spirit of the universe, of which every man is a part. In order to "realize" this, Unity advocates the repetition of such statements as this:

> I am the Son of God, and the Spirit of the most High dwells in me:
> I am the Christ of God.
> He who hath seen me hath seen the Father.
> I and my Father are one.[5]

There is some ambiguity concerning evil, which at times seems to exist, and at times is denied existence. At any rate, sickness and disease are the result of inward conditions, conquerable by the ancient yogic method of concentration upon the fact that the individual soul is one with the Infinite.

3. Charles Samuel Braden, *These Also Believe* (New York: Macmillan, 1949), p. 157.
4. In Ibid.
5. Charles Fillmore, *The Science of Being and Christian Healing* (Kansas City, Mo.: Unity Tract Society, 1920), pp. 27-28.

Ultimate salvation is connected with the belief in reincarnation, and is attained when the cycle of birth is
broken and man comes to birth no more. As expressed in
Unity's statement of faith, "We believe that the dissolution of spirit, soul, and body caused by death, is annulled
by rebirth of the same spirit and soul in another body here
on earth. We believe the repeated incarnations of man to
be a merciful provision of our loving Father to the end that
all may have opportunity to attain immortality through regeneration, as did Jesus."

## THE "I AM" MOVEMENT

A CURSORY READING of *The "I AM" Decrees* reveals that
there is little if anything new in this system. A central concept is that of the Ascended Masters who are the custo-
dians of the "Eternal Inner Understanding" of the "I AM,
the Great Creative Word." The Ascended Master, Saint
Germain, is chief among thousands, and is the one through
whom this teaching came to its founders.

The conception of God is pantheistic. "Life in all its
activities everywhere manifest, is *God in Action,* and it is
only through lack of understanding of applied thought and
feeling that mankind is constantly interrupting" the pure
flow of that Perfect Essence of Life, "I AM" is the Activity
of "That Life."[1] "When you say and feel 'I AM,' you release the spring of Eternal, Everlasting Life, to flow on its
way unmolested. In other words, you open wide the door
to Its natural flow. . . . 'I AM' is the Full Activity of God."[2]
The repetition of the words "I AM" is to bring the experiential realization that there is no other being besides oneself. "The student is admonished to look always, and never
forget it, to his own God Self, which is the Creator of his in-

1. Godfré Ray King, *The "I AM" Discourses* (Chicago: St. Germain
   Press, 1936), p. 2.
2. Ibid., pp. 2-3.

dividualization."[3] "When the student can once understand that the Ascended Host of Masters are but the more advanced consciousness of himself, then he will begin to feel the unquestionable possibilities within his grasp. Whether he speaks to the Godhead direct, to one of the Ascended Masters of Light or to his own God Self, in reality it makes no difference, for all are One. Until one does reach this state of consciousness, it does make a difference, for the individual is almost certain to feel a division of the One Self, which is not possible to be made, except in the ignorance of the outer activity of the mind."[4] For this reason there is no sickness, for divinity cannot be sick.

Man is on the cosmic wheel of existence, and can only escape by the comprehension of the truth as given. Any one who dies without grasping the truth of the Law of Life must return in another body and try again to secure the victory.

## BAHAISM

BAHAISM DIFFERS from all other cults discussed in that its roots are in Islam. It is, however, quite un-Islamic in its lack of positive dogma and in its eclecticism. Bahaism claims to be the fulfillment of past revelations of the world's major religions. It "upholds the unity of God, recognizes the unity of His Prophets, and inculcates the principle of the oneness and wholeness of the entire human race."[1]

The first recognized founder was known as The Bab, or "Gate," and lived in Persia. In 1844 he proclaimed himself the messenger whose coming had been foretold by Muhammad. His successor was known as Baha'u'llah, "The Glory of God." He declared, "plainly and repeatedly, that he was the long-expected educator and teacher of all peo-

3. Ibid., p. 27.
4. Ibid., p. 28.
1. Shoghi Effendi, *The Faith of Baha'u'llah* (Wilmette, Ill.: Baha'i Publishing Trust, 1959), pp. 7-8.

ples, the channel of a wondrous Grace that would tran-
scend all previous outpourings, in which all previous forms
of religion would be merged, as rivers merge in the ocean."[2]
He was to bring about the inauguration of the glorious age
of peace on earth foretold by prophets of old. It would be
characterized by unity of mankind, religions, races, nations; equality of men and women; unification of languages; one international tribunal for judgment of all. The
Baha'i World Faith is named after Baha'u'llah. With him
it was claimed, "the Prophetic Cycle hath verily ended.
The Eternal Truth is now come."[3]

It is singular that out of the dogmatism of inflexible
Islam should come a religion which teaches that all religions are one. The concept of deity is at times Islamic,
and at other times it savors of pantheism. No member of
the human family is bad, or evil. "Sin" is defined as the absence of good in the life of the faithful. Therefore atonement is unnecessary. "Education will free men from all im-
perfections."[4] The founders of all major religions were
messengers of God by whom the evolution of human society has progressed. Baha'u'llah is the voice of God for
this age. In him the culmination has been reached.

## SWEDENBORGIANISM—THE CHURCH OF
## THE NEW JERUSALEM

CALLED "THE NEW CHURCH" BY ITS MEMBERS, Sweden-
borgianism, or The Church of the New Jerusalem, takes
its unique teachings from the religious writings of Emanuel Swedenborg (1688-1772). He was a noted scientist
and philosopher who devoted the last thirty years of his
life to "a comprehensive restatement of the Christian message." This study followed a "profound religious experi-

2. J. E. Esslemont, *Baha'u'llah and the New Era* (Wilmette, Ill.:
   Baha'i Publishing Committee, 1948), p. 7.
3. *Baha'i World Faith: Selected Writings of Baha'u'llah and Abdu'l
   Baha* (Wilmette, Ill.: Baha'i Publishing Trust, 1956), title page.
4. Ibid., p. 319.

ence which was accompanied by an opening of his consciousness into the world of spirit."[1] His Latin volumes
of doctrinal and biblical interpretation and other-world
disclosures number more than thirty.

The Church of the New Jerusalem was organized in London in 1787. It claims to be a Protestant church, founded
upon the Bible, with its central teaching about "the Lord
God." However, a better evaluation is found in the statement that "we are a teaching church, seeking to make
Christian theology understood and reasonable to the en-
quiring mind."[2] In fundamental doctrines, Swedenborgian-
ism is utterly at odds with orthodox Christianity. Sufficient
to prove this are these statements from Swedenborg's *True
Christian Religion:*

> The passion of the cross was the last temptation which
> the Lord, as the greatest Prophet, endured; also it was a
> means of glorifying His Human, that is, of uniting it with
> the Divine of the Father; but it was not redemption.[3]
> The belief that the passion of the cross was redemption
> itself is a fundamental error of the church; and this error,
> together with the error respecting three Divine Persons
> from eternity, has perverted the whole church so that
> nothing spiritual is left in it.[4]

The "final judgment" took place in 1757, at which time
the "new dispensation" began. Since then the Lord has
been engaged in "performing a redemption" which pertains to the subjugation of the hells and establishment of
order in the heavens. This is in preparation for a new spiritual church.

In rejecting the orthodox doctrine of the Trinity, Swe-

1. Explanatory card issued by Church of the Holy City, Washington, D.C.
2. Bulletin of the Church of the Holy City, Washington, D.C.
3. Emanuel Swedenborg, *True Christian Religion* (Boston and New York: Houghton Mifflin, 1949), 1:175.
4. Ibid.

denborg taught that God exists in His one person in three
ways:

God in the depths of His Being is the Father;
God knowable and known is the Son;
God actively and always engaged in imparting of Him-
self is the Holy Spirit.

Christ is believed to have inherited evil from his mother.
But "God has revealed Himself most completely in the
person of Jesus Christ who overcame the limitations of His
human nature until He became one with God."[5]
The efficacy of the cross having been set aside, the bodily resurrection is denied. It is declared that "the Lord
Jesus Christ appeared to the spiritually alert senses of the
disciples as the very same beloved Lord and Master whom
they thought had 'died' on the cross."[6] The regeneration
mentioned in the third chapter of John is a spiritual matter, and in that sense we are reborn every time a new affection possesses us. Man lives on earth only once. This
one existence determines character, and the character established here in life is maintained in the hereafter. At
death, the person enters a "world of spirits," which is a
state between heaven and hell. There two ways of life
are presented to every person. The choice is a free one,
for "our Lord said, 'I judge no man.'" Actually the judgment seat is in our own hearts, for we judge ourselves by
the choices we make. In the world of spirits the selfish
and vile man may change, but unfortunately we tend to
react on the basis of past reactions. The good man seeks
more of what is good and true; the sinner finds boon com-
panions. And so we pass on to the Further Life. Spiritual
failures go to the environment suited to their natures, in
bondage to insatiable desires. "All-consuming passions con-

5. Bulletin of the Church of the Holy City, Washington, D.C.
6. *Life Further On* (Philadelphia: American New-Church Tract and
Publishing Society, n.d.), p. 28.

tinue to burn, and to leave him frustrated. That is hell."[7]
Heaven is the place where the fundamentally honest man
finds his like. It is a real world, with cities, churches,
schools, homes, and gardens; and it is filled with men and
women who have cultivated the fine things of life, each
doing what he is most interested in doing and can do best.
It is a society of redeemed men and women—a human
achievement.

## ROSICRUCIANISM (THE ROSE CROSS)

THE ORDER OF ROSICRUCIANS was founded in 1313 by Chris
Rosenkreuz. Its adherents see in the cross a symbol of
"the life currents vitalizing the bodies of plants, animals,
and man." The founder felt that his mission was to prepare a new phase of the Christian religion for the coming
age (in which we now live) in order to keep pace with
the normal progress in evolution. It is claimed that the
philosophy is entirely Christian, "striving to lead to Christ
those who cannot find Him by faith alone."[1] It seeks to
foster the acceptance of Christian doctrines through the
medium of esoteric knowledge. This knowledge is that
which has been acquired from the ancients of Egypt, India,
Tibet, Mexico, and other places.

The basic textbook is the *Rosicrucian Cosmo-Conception*, by Max Heindel. It is known as the Western Wisdom,
given to the author by the elder Brothers of the Rose Cross.
*Cosmo-Conception* "gives the most logical explanation of
the universe and man's part in it from the viewpoint of evolution ever issued to the general public. The earlier ages
vaguely referred to in Genesis are fully elucidated, show-
ing how man started as a spark of the Divine Flame of God,
and after aeons of preparation reached his present state,
and will finally attain the perfection of superman."[2]

7. Ibid., p. 25.
1. *The Rosicrucian Interpretation of Christianity* (Oceanside, Calif.:
Rosicrucian Fellowship, n.d.), p. 1.
2. Advertisement of Rosicrucian Fellowship, Oceanside, Calif.

There are currently two active organizations with the same teaching: The Rosicrucian Fellowship, in Oceanside, California, and the Ancient Mystical Order Rosae Crucis, known as AMORC, with headquarters in San Jose, California. The latter organization emphasizes that the Rosicrucians are *not* a religious organization, but "a non-sectarian fraternity devoted to the investigation and study of the higher principles of life as found expressed in man and nature."[3] It is interesting to note that the claimed connection with Egypt came through the acceptance of some of the fundamental teachings of the Gnostics and the Pythagorians. AMORC is strictly secret, spiritual, and free from dogma so that members of all religions may become acolytes. It is not a separate religion but fundamentally religious, teaching the immortality of the soul and the fatherhood of God.

The motto is "Try." One is saved not by another's intervention or substitution but by overcoming all evil. Everyone possesses an incorruptible seed, a divine spark, a Christos, which must be awakened and brought into consciousness. Christ is not the only begotten Son of God. He returns to earth every year, and offers a sacrifice. All will attain perfection by the normal process of reincarnation, although some will progress faster than others. The Law of Sowing and Reaping, the Hindu Karma, is operative in every life.

The centers of the orders carry on various activities. There are studies in philosophy, astrology, healing, printing, and Bible study. In certain areas the teaching is similar to that of Theosophy. There are the Seven Worlds, separated not by space or distance but by rate of vibrations. There are Invisible Helpers, who work on the spiritual planes to bring healing by raising the vibrations of the sick to higher levels. The appeal of Rosicrucianism is largely through its accent on the occult and the mysterious.

3. Letterhead of International Supreme Temple, San Jose, Calif.

# Bibliography

## GENERAL

Bach, Marcus. *They Have Found a Faith*. Indianapolis: Bobbs-Merrill, 1946.

Braden, Charles Samuel. *These Also Believe*. New York: Macmillan, 1949.

Ferm, Virgilius, ed. *Religion in the Twentieth Century*. New York: Philosophical Library, 1948.

Gerstner, John H. *The Theology of the Major Sects*. Grand Rapids: Baker, 1960.

Hoekema, Anthony A. *The Four Major Cults*. Grand Rapids: Eerdmans, 1963.

Lewis, Gordon R. *Confronting the Cults*. Nutley, N.J.: Presby. & Ref., 1966.

Sanders, J. Oswald. *Cults and Isms*. Grand Rapids: Zondervan, 1962.

Spittler, Russell P. *Cults and Isms*. Grand Rapids: Baker, 1962.

## MORMONISM

The Book of Mormon. Salt Lake City: The Church of Jesus Christ of Latter-day Saints.

Doctrine and Covenants. Salt Lake City: The Church of Jesus Christ of Latter-day Saints.

Fraser, Gordon H. *Is Mormonism Christian?* Rev. ed. Chicago: Moody, 1977.

McConkie, Bruce R. *Mormon Doctrine*. Salt Lake City: Bookcraft, 1966.

Morgan, John. *The Plan of Salvation*. Salt Lake City: Deseret (pamphlet).

169

The Pearl of Great Price. Salt Lake City: The Church of Jesus
     Christ of Latter-day Saints.
Peterson, Mark E. *Which Church Is Right?* Salt Lake City:
     Deseret, n.d. (pamphlet).
Smith, Elbert A. *Differences That Persist.* Independence, Mo.:
     Herald Publishing House (publishing house of The Reorgan-
     ized Church of Jesus Christ of Latter Day Saints).
Smith, Joseph F. *Gospel Doctrine.* Salt Lake City: Deseret,
     1963.
Smith, Joseph Fielding. *Teachings of the Prophet Joseph Smith.*
     Salt Lake City: Deseret, 1958. Excerpts from sermons and
     writings of Joseph Smith.
Talmage, James E. *A Study of the Articles of Faith.* Salt Lake
     City: The Church of Jesus Christ of Latter-day Saints, 1961.
Tanner, Jerald, and Tanner, Sandra. *The Changing World of
     Mormonism.* Chicago: Moody, 1979.
*Uniform System for Teaching Investigators.* Salt Lake City:
     Deseret. Published for use only by Mormon missionaries.
Young, Brigham. *Journal of Discourses.* Liverpool, 1854-75.

### JEHOVAH'S WITNESSES

*Let God Be True.* Brooklyn: Watchtower Bible and Tract
     Society, 1952.
*Make Sure of All Things.* Brooklyn: Watchtower Bible and
     Tract Society, 1953.
*New Heavens and a New Earth.* Brooklyn: Watchtower Bible
     and Tract Society, 1953.
*New World Translation of the Holy Scriptures.* Brooklyn:
     Watchtower Bible and Tract Society, 1961.
*Studies in the Scriptures.* 7 vols. Allegheny, Pa.: Watchtower
     Bible and Tract Society.
*The Word—Who is He?* Brooklyn: Watchtower Bible and Tract
     Society.

### UNIFICATION CHURCH

Moon, Sun Myung. *Christianity in Crisis.* Washington, D.C.:
     Holy Spirit Association for the Unification of World Chris-
     tianity, 1974.

———. *The Divine Principle.* Washington, D.C.: Holy Spirit Association for the Unification of World Christianity, 1973.

Sontag, Frederick. *Sun Myung Moon.* Nashville: Abingdon, 1977.

Yamamoto, J. Isamu. *The Puppet Master.* Downers Grove, Ill.: InterVarsity, 1977.


## WORLDWIDE CHURCH OF GOD

Armstrong, Herbert W. *All About Water Baptism.* Pasadena, Calif.: Ambassador College Press, 1954.

———. *Does God Heal Today?* Pasadena, Calif.: Ambassador College Press, 1952.

———. *Lazarus and the Rich Man.* Pasadena, Calif.: Radio Church of God, 1953.

———. *Predestination—Does the Bible Teach It?* Pasadena, Calif.: Radio Church of God, 1957.

———. *The United States and the British Commonwealth in Prophecy.* Pasadena, Calif.: Ambassador College Press, 1954.

———. *Which Day Is the Sabbath of the New Testament?* Pasadena, Calif.: Ambassador College Press, 1952.

Benware, Paul N. *Ambassadors of Armstrongism.* Nutley, N.J.: Presby. & Ref., 1975.

Hopkins, Joseph. *The Armstrong Empire.* Grand Rapids: Eerdmans, 1974.


## THE WAY INTERNATIONAL

Whiteside, Elena S. *The Way: Living in Love.* New Knoxville, Ohio: American Christian Press, 1972.

Wierwille, Victor Paul. *The Bible Tells Me So.* Studies in Abundant Living, vol. 1. New Knoxville, Ohio: American Christian Press, 1971.

———. *Jesus Christ Is Not God.* New Knoxville, Ohio: American Christian Press, 1975.

———. *The New, Dynamic Church.* Studies in Abundant Living, vol. 2. New Knoxville, Ohio: American Christian Press, 1971.

——. *The Word's Way*. Studies in Abundant Living, vol. 3. New Knoxville, Ohio: American Christian Press, 1971.
Williams, J. L. *Victor Paul Wierwille and the Way International*. Chicago: Moody, 1979.

## EASTERN MYSTICISM

Braden, Charles Samuel. *The Scriptures of Mankind: An Introduction.* New York: Macmillan, 1952.
Cameron, Charles, ed. *Who is Guru Maharaj Ji?* New York: Bantam, 1973.
Isherwood, Christopher, ed. *Vedanta for Modern Man.* New York: Collier, 1962.
Noss, John B. *Man's Religions*. New York: Macmillan, 1956.
Prabhavananda Swami, and Isherwood, Christopher, trans. *Bhagavad-Gita: Song of God*. New York: Mentor Classic, 1951.
Yogi, Maharishi Mahesh. *Meditations of Maharishi Mahesh Yogi*. New York: Bantam, 1973.

## SCIENTOLOGY

Garrison, Omar. *The Hidden Story of Scientology*. London: Arlington, 1914.

## CHRISTIAN SCIENCE

Dakin, Edwin F. *Mrs. Eddy, the Biography of a Virginal Mind*. New York: Scribner's, 1930.
Eddy, Mary Baker. *Miscellaneous Writings, 1883-1896*. Boston: Allison V. Stewart, 1910.
——. *No and Yes*. Boston: Allison V. Stewart, for the trustees under the will of Mary Baker Eddy, 1910.
——. *Rudimental Divine Science*. Boston: The trustees under the will of Mary Baker Eddy, 1908.
——. *Science and Health with Key to the Scriptures*. Boston: Allison V. Stewart, for the trustees under the will of Mary Baker Eddy. First published in 1875.

### SPIRITUALISM

Austin, B. F. *The ABC of Spiritualism*. Milwaukee: National Spiritualist Association of Churches, n.d.
*The Spiritualist Manual*, 9th rev. Milwaukee: National Spiritualist Association of Churches, 1955.

### THEOSOPHY

Besant, Annie. *Popular Lectures on Theosophy*. Chicago: Rajput Press, 1910.
——. *Theosophy*. London and Edinburgh: T. C. & E. C. Jack, n.d.
Blavatsky, H. P. *The Key to Theosophy*. 1889. Reprint. Covina, Calif.: Theosophical University Press, 1946.
Leadbeater, C. W. *An Outline of Theosophy*. Chicago: Theosophical Book Concern, 1903.

### UNITY SCHOOL OF CHRISTIANITY

Fillmore, Charles. *The Science of Being and Christian Healing*. Kansas City, Mo.: Unity Tract Society, 1920.

### "I AM" MOVEMENT

*The "I AM" Decrees*. Los Angeles: Sindelar Studios, 1931.
King, Godfré Ray. *The "I AM" Discourses*. Chicago: St. Germain Press, 1936.

### BAHAISM

*Baha'i World Faith: Selected Writings of Baha'u'llah and Abdu'l Baha*. Wilmette, Ill.: Baha'i Publishing Trust, 1956.
Effendi, Shoghi. *The Faith of Baha'u'llah*. Wilmette, Ill.: Baha'i Publishing Trust, 1959.
Esslemont, J. E. *Baha'u'llah and the New Era*. Wilmette, Ill.: Baha'i Publishing Committee, 1948.
Sohrab, Mirza Ahmad. *Broken Silence*. New York: Universal Publishing, 1942.

## Swedenborgianism

Keller, Helen. *My Religion.* New York: Avon, 1927.

*Life Further On.* Philadelphia: American New-Church Tract and Publishing Society (booklet).

Swedenborg, Emanuel. *Emanuel Swedenborg's Works.* 21 vols. Boston and New York: Houghton Mifflin.

———. *True Christian Religion.* Boston and New York: Houghton Mifflin, 1949.

## Rosicrucianism

*The Confederation of Initiates.* Quakertown, Pa.: Fraternitatis Rosae Crucis, Dept. of Instruction, Beverly Hall.

Heindel, Max. *Rosicrucian Cosmo-Conception.* 23rd ed. London: L. N. Fowler, 1956.

*The Rosicrucian Digest.* San Jose, Calif. Official magazine of the Ancient Mystical Order Rosae Crucis (AMORC).

*The Rosicrucian Interpretation of Christianity.* Oceanside, Calif.: Rosicrucian Fellowship.

*The Rosicrucian Magazine.* Oceanside, Calif. Official publication of The Rosicrucian Fellowship.

*The Science of Death.* Oceanside, Calif.: The Rosicrucian Fellowship.

*The Secret Schools.* Quakertown, Pa.: Fraternitatis Rosae Crucis, Dept. of Instruction, Beverly Hall.